Bank Notes

Series editor **David Palfreman**
Senior Lecturer,
Central Manchester College

This series provides a structured revision programme for students taking their Institute of Bankers Stage 2 Banking Diploma examinations.

By answering a series of Short Answer Tests at the front of the book, students can decide on their revision priorities. Taking one topic at a time, they can refresh their knowledge of the topic using the Study Guide, and then test themselves using the Multiple Choice Questions. Most importantly, detailed notes on *all* answers to the Multiple Choice Questions are given, so that students can reinforce their learning by discovering why wrong answers *are* wrong.

Finally, by tackling the Post-tests for each topic, students can test the effectiveness of their revision.

There are eight titles in the series:

Law Relating to Banking
Monetary Economics
Accountancy
Investment
Nature of Management
Finance of International Trade
Practice of Banking 1
Practice of Banking 2

INSTITUTE OF BANKERS
STAGE 2 BANKING DIPLOMA

Law Relating to Banking

D PALFREMAN

Van Nostrand Reinhold (UK) Co. Ltd

First published in 1986 by
Van Nostrand Reinhold (UK) Co. Ltd
Molly Millars Lane, Wokingham, Berkshire,
England

Typeset in Ehrhardt 10 on 11½ point by
Columns Ltd, Reading

Printed and bound in Great Britain by
Billing & Sons Ltd, Worcester

ISBN 0 442 31739 5

Contents

Editor's Introduction — vii

How to use this book — xv

Short Answer Tests

Questions — 2

Answers — 8

Topics

Topic 1 *Banker and Customer*
Study Guide — 26
Multiple Choice Questions — 29
Answers — 32

Topic 2 *The Law of Agency*
Study Guide — 36
Multiple Choice Questions — 40
Answers — 43

Topic 3 *Partnership*
Study Guide — 48
Multiple Choice Questions — 55
Answers — 58

Topic 4 *Companies*
Study Guide — 62
Multiple Choice Questions — 69
Answers — 72

Topic 5 *Bankruptcy*
Study Guide — 78
Multiple Choice Questions — 85
Answers — 88

Topic 6 *Land and its Use as Security*
Study Guide — 93
Multiple Choice Questions — 100
Answers — 103

Topic 7 *Life Assurance Policies and Stocks and Shares*
Study Guide — 107

Contents

Multiple Choice Questions   113
Answers   116

Topic 8 *Guarantees*
Study Guide   121
Multiple Choice Questions   127
Answers   130

Topic 9 *Bills of Exchange*
Study Guide   136
Multiple Choice Questions   145
Answers   148

Topic 10 *Cheques*
Study Guide   152
Multiple Choice Questions   160
Answers   163

Post-tests

Questions   169
Answers   196

Editor's Introduction

What's this book about?

This book will help you pass your Institute of Bankers examination. Interested? Well, read on and you'll see how.

You're probably at the stage in your studies when you've got information coming out of your ears, a huge file of notes and the exam looming ever nearer! Quite possibly, you're beginning to get that familiar feeling of desperation: 'Where do I start?', 'I'll never learn all this.'

Help is at hand. If you use this book properly you'll discover where you should start and you'll learn more efficiently. Perhaps this will be the first time you'll have approached study in a methodical, effective fashion. By the way, we won't be throwing a whole lot of new information at you — you probably know quite enough already; there's nothing in this book which you shouldn't already know or, perhaps, knew once but have forgotten! Our aim is to help you understand, learn and use it.

So you want to pass the exam . . .

Well, your study should be: *positive*, *efficient*, and *effective*. Remember two *key ideas*:
— *Organization*
— *Activity*

Organization

Let's explain what we mean. *How well organized are you?* Do you waste time looking for things, do you spend as long getting ready to do something as actually doing it? How many times have we seen students ploughing through a thoroughly disorganized file to find something? What a waste of time! The point is made, we think; so get yourself organized.

Time: When are you going to study? Only you know when you've the time and only you know when you work best. For example, are you a 'lark' or an 'owl'? Be realistic. It's no good trying to revise for a few minutes here and there, while the adverts are on, for example. You must commit a *realistic* amount of time to any one session — probably not less than one hour and not more than three.

Have you ever thought of formally timetabling your study? Look at the timetable shown. You could draw similar ones (one for each week) and mark in your revision times.

As you can see, the timetable caters for both 'larks' and 'owls', as well as for all tendencies in between. Clearly there'll be major blocks of time when you can't do any study — you have to go to work — but that still leaves a lot of available time. Make the best use of it. A word of warning, however: if you have long-standing or important domestic or leisure commitments, think twice about breaking them. At least try first to build them into your timetable.

Study Timetable

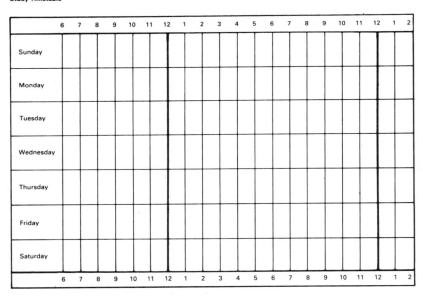

Place: The kitchen table or the sofa in front of the TV are *not* the ideal places to work. You need to be able to concentrate and this means finding somewhere *reasonably quiet* — don't try to revise with the Hi-Fi on! Equally important you need somewhere which is *comfortable*: a good chair, a desk or table, and good lighting. Ideally, you should be able to leave your work out, ready to come back to, so that you don't waste time at the start of your next session — one reason why the kitchen table isn't suitable.

Pace: Contrary to popular practice, it's *not* a good idea to leave revision to the last minute, particularly if you want to revise positively, efficiently and effectively.

Plan your revision: We've included some short answer tests which you should complete before reading the rest of the book. These exercises will help you identify your own strengths and weaknesses and so help you to determine how long you need to spend on each topic.

Use your study timetable to plan a revision campaign. Believe me, the more carefully you plan, the more you'll get done in any given time. Of course, you're bound to end up working like crazy for the few days immediately before the exam, so you might as well plan for this as well! What must not happen, and a planned revision campaign will prevent this, is finding that you haven't allocated your time properly and that there's just no way you're going to be able to study everything thoroughly in time.

Activity

How long can you concentrate on any one thing? If you're honest, not very long. And when it comes to revision, let's face it, it really takes the prize in the boredom stakes. No one likes to just sit there trying to learn something. But don't despair — there are ways to make it more bearable and effective. Read on.

What you should not do is sit there reading the same original notes over and over again. It's not only excrutiatingly boring, it's also very unproductive. After you've read your notes through once, you'll find you know much of what you're reading already and progressively more of your time will be wasted each time you repeat the exercise.

Bank notes: *Be active*, and this is where the *Bank Notes* series comes into its own. If you use each book properly (see *How to use this book* on p. xv) you'll find yourself very active in your study. In particular, you'll be interacting with the subject matter instead of being a passive, and not particularly absorbant, sponge.

Your aims: Remember, however, that this series is not a substitute for your own hard work; you'll still have to put in *time* and *effort*. Your study should have three aims:
— Complete *understanding of the topic.*
— *Retention* and *recall* of it.
— The ability to *explain* and *apply* what you have learnt.

Study activities: So, a few general suggestions for *study activities*, all tried and tested, to achieve these aims. You'll find further ideas and guidance in the Study Guides to the Topics.

Revision Notes: Your course notes and text books are not particularly suitable to revise from. Making revision notes is a good investment of your time. They can consist of just the headings in your notes/text book with, perhaps, a brief note about important principles or unusual points.

Do take care in the way you lay out your notes. Don't try to economize on paper; it's probably the lowest of your overheads anyway! Your notes should look 'attractive' and be easy to follow. Allow space to add other brief comments later. Try the following as a model:

MAIN HEADING
SUB-HEADING
....

Sub-sub-Heading
....

1. Important point...
....
2. Important point...
....

When you've made your revision notes, you can use them in the following way. Take each note in turn and try to recall and explain the subject matter. If you can, go on to the next; if you can't look back to your notes/text book — perhaps noting a page number for future reference. By doing this, you'll revise, test your knowledge and generally spend your time productively by concentrating your revision on those aspects of the subject with which you're least familiar. In addition, you'll have an excellent last-minute revision aid.

Summary diagrams: These could be alternatives or additions to revision notes. Many people respond well to diagrammatic explanations and summaries; in particular, the visual association of the different aspects of a subject is useful.

We've two specific types of diagrams in mind: the 'family tree' type and the 'molecule' type, as you'll see below. Of course, if you've seen or can devise other types, use those as well.

Constructing diagrams is a particularly useful form of active study because you have to think how best to construct them and in so doing you'll find you better understand the subject. As with revision notes, don't include too much on each diagram and don't economise on paper. The impact and usefulness of a diagram depends very much on its visual simplicity.

You can use summary diagrams in much the same way as revision notes.

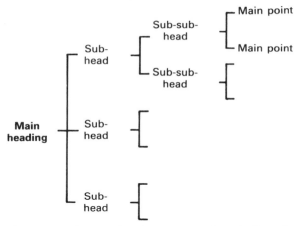

'Family tree' summary diagram (can be constructed vertically or horizontally, as here).

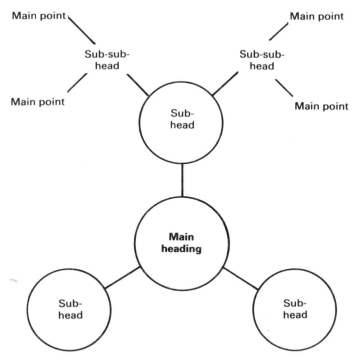

'Molecule' summary diagram.

Useful definitions and explanations: Each subject has a handful of points that are almost certain to come up in at least one question in the exam. So, why not prepare for them? (The *Study Guides* will suggest what these could be.) In practical terms, you may save yourself two or three minutes on each question simply because you don't have to think about how to define or explain something which you probably know well but cannot easily put into words there and then. Multiplied five times, those two or three minutes represent a considerable time saving. We've all wished for another 10–15 minutes in the exam before now!

Plan answers to past questions: Plan them, don't answer them fully. Once you've planned an answer, the writing out is largely a mechanical exercise. If, however, you feel you need the practice, answer some fully.

Examination technique

At this stage in your studies, there's not much we can say to give you a better answering technique. However, there are a number of general points you should remember about actual exam technique.

— *Read the instructions carefully.* You get no extra marks for answering an extra question and you automatically lose a proportion of the possible marks by answering too few. Also, answer the right number of questions from each section. Basic points, perhaps, but you would not believe . . .

— *Read all the questions through* and provisionally select which questions to answer. Be careful in your choice; an apparently simple question may have a hidden twist — don't get caught. Similarly, in a multi-part question be sure you can answer all parts and not just the first.

— Everyone suffers from *exam nerves* and these will probably affect you for the first fifteen minutes or so. Consequently, it's often good practice to answer your 'best' question second or third. By that time you'll be thoroughly relaxed and working well.

— *Plan all your answers* — this is absolutely vital.

— *Divide your time more or less equally between questions.* There's no point spending an extra 15 minutes on your best question if it results in a very poor final question.

— *Check through your answers.* If you spend a few minutes doing this at the end of the exam, you can eliminate minor errors and give a final 'polish' to your answers. When allocating your time, allow five minutes for this.

What do I do now?

You may have been fortunate in your studies and have been taught some or all of the techniques outlined above. If you were, you should now be doubly persuaded of their effectiveness. If you weren't, you've already invested your time well because you're virtually guaranteed to perform better in the exam through having used them than you would otherwise have done.

Back to *Bank Notes*, and where they fit in. We've talked about being 'organized' and 'active' and we've given you a sound set of general ideas as a start. *Bank Notes* go further; not only do they provide an organized and active structure for study, they are also your *personal revision tutor*. Now turn to *How to use this Book* on page xv and start your revision campaign.

How to use this book

At any time in your revision campaign is the simple answer, but the earlier the better. Because we've designed the book to identify any weak areas you may have, and suggest positive ideas to help you study and revise, you'll find this book the ideal basis on which to plan that revision campaign. However, it's equally useful just before the exam when some self-assessment and new revision activities may well revive the flagging spirit!

The different sections

You'll find that this book has *five* sections:

— *Editor's Introduction*: a short but very important section which gives you tried and tested advice on how to revise positively, efficiently and effectively. If you haven't read it, go back and read it now and *only then continue with this section.*

— *How to use this Book*: the section you're reading now.

— *Short Answer Tests*: designed to help you identify your strengths and weaknesses in this subject.

— Ten *Topic Sections*: broadly following the order of the Institute's syllabus and containing:
an overview of and advice on how best to revise each of the topics,
Multiple choice questions and full explanatory answers designed both to test and to teach.

— *Post-tests*: designed to help you assess the effectiveness of your revision and identify any remaining weaknesses.

The short answer tests

You start with these; there's one test for each main section of the syllabus. Complete them all before you go on to the *Topic Sections*. Each test is scored out of 20 and we've allocated marks to the questions — usually two marks to each — and explained in the answers how to score. These tests will quickly give you a good idea of how much you know. By filling in the *Score Grid* — you'll find it inside the back cover — you'll be able to compare your knowledge and understanding on the different parts of the syllabus and identify your revision priorities.

Remember what we said about the value of organization? The *Score Grid* provides an effective chart on which not only to identify and order your revision priorities but also to plot the progress of your revision campaign and assess its efficiency. Look at the *Score Grid* now, and then turn back to here.

The topic sections

When you've completed all ten *Short Answer Tests*, filled in the *Score Grid* and determined the order of your revision, you can turn to the *Topic Sections*.

Study Guides: These, if you like, are your personal revision tutor. Each gives you an overview of the topic and a study framework. We indicate the points you really must know and be able to explain and use, and we point out common student mistakes and give advice on how best to tackle each topic. Some sections already contain revision notes and summary diagrams — remember the *Editor's Introduction* — and you can use these as guides for your further work. For example, if you're given a diagram which summarizes the entire topic, you could take each of the sub-sub-headings in that diagram, use them as main headings and produce more detailed diagrams on those particular parts of the topic.

You can also combine these introductions with the more general advice on study we've already given you. So, you should find that the *Study Guides* form the bases for very thorough revision campaigns on the topics.

Multiple-Choice Questions: You've probably answered 'MCQ' tests before. Such questions are an excellent way of testing knowledge and understanding but the feedback from the tutor is usually minimal, often non-existent. You don't usually know why your answer was right or wrong. Here's where the *Bank Notes* series is different.

It's through the MCQs that the books start to *work with you* to remedy your weaknesses in the different topics and reinforce the knowledge and understanding you already have.

For each question we've given you four possible answers; all are plausible and, indeed, all may be partially correct but only one is totally correct. After each question there's a space to put your answer — a, b, c, or d. You could also briefly write down the reason you chose that answer, just to stop yourself succumbing to the temption of guessing!

When you've finished all the MCQs for a topic, turn to the

answers — they follow immediately — and mark your own answers. You score two marks for each correct answer. (Keep a note of your score at the end of the test and enter it on the Score Grid.) We don't just tell you whether you're right or wrong in the answers — we give you a full explanation of why. You'll find these explanations very useful; quite probably the 'penny will drop' where it didn't before.

References to other books: At this point in your studies you might feel it's a bit late to start reading text books! You've probably had enough of them anyway. However, if you consider that you need to do some more reading on a particular point you'll find the books listed below useful. Sometimes we give you a specific reference but a quick look at a contents page or in an index will find you what you want.

We think you'll find the following books useful on this subject:

Law of Banking, Palfreman, Pitman.
Banking Law, Hamblin, Sweet & Maxwell.
The Law Relating to Banking, Reeday, Butterworth.

The post-tests

The final section consists of 10 *post-tests*. These also use MCQs but this time you're just told which answer is correct.

You'll find that the post-tests largely retest what was covered in the main MCQs. This is deliberate. The purpose of the post-tests is to assess the progress you've made in your revision campaign.

You may wish to answer them all together — a kind of mock exam if you like — and record your scores — *two* marks for each correct answer — on the Score Grid. You can then compare your score with those on the corresponding Short Answer Test and Main MCQ Test. While the comparisons won't be 'scientific', you will get a good indication of the effectiveness of your revision.

What do I do when I've finished?

If you work through this book properly and revise conscientiously following our guidance, you should be well prepared for the exam. However, if the post-tests reveal that you still have some areas of weakness you'll have to go back and revise these again — at least you'll know which ones they are and how to go about it!

Finally, remember our general advice on exam technique. The best of luck; we're sure you'll do well.

David Palfreman *Editor/Author*

Short Answer Tests

Start your revision by attempting the short answer tests on pages 2 to 7.

Questions

Topic 1 Banker and customer

1 State the three activities the performance of which are regarded as the criteria for determining status as a banker. (*3 marks*)
2 Is a course of dealings with a banker necessary to establish a person as the customer of that banker? (*1 mark*)
3 What is the basic legal nature of the banker–customer relationship: (*2 marks*)
4 What principle was established in *Lloyds Bank v. Bundy* (1975)? (*2 marks*)
5 State the principle established in *London Joint Stock Bank v. Macmillan & Arthur* (1918). (*2 marks*)
6 What is meant by the right of set-off? (*2 marks*)
7 State two exceptions to a banker's general duty not to disclose information about his customers' affairs. (*2 marks*)
8 Is a banker who accepts his customer's property into safe custody the bailor or the bailee of that property? (*2 marks*)
9 What principle was established in *Hedley Byrne & Co. v. Heller Partners* (1963)? (*2 marks*)
10 Does a customer owe a duty to check bank statements and inform the bank of any inaccuracy in them? (*2 marks*)

Answers on page 8

Topic 2 The law of agency

1 What is an agent's main function? (*2 marks*)
2 Distinguish between a general and a special agent. (*2 marks*)
3 Name the four ways in which agency can be created. (*2 marks*)
4 Name four duties of an agent. (*2 marks*)
5 If an agent buys goods on behalf of his principal and is given a trade discount by the supplier, is the agent entitled to keep the discount? (*2 marks*)
6 In what circumstances can an agent appoint a sub-agent? (*2 marks*)
7 When an agent signs a bill of exchange, what must he do to ensure he does not incur personal liability on the bill? (*2 marks*)
8 What is the rule in *Collen v. Wright* (1856)? (*2 marks*)
9 Give an example of a situation in which agency may be irrevocable. (*2 marks*)

10 Give two examples of the law of agency being directly relevant to banking. (*2 marks*)

Answers on page 9

Topic 3   Partnership

1 Define a partnership. (*2 marks*)
2 What is the principal legal distinction between a partnership and a registered company? (*2 marks*)
3 Many partnerships operate under a firm name. What disclosure requirements are laid down by the Business Names Act 1985 for such partnerships? (*2 marks*)
4 How does a limited partner differ from an ordinary partner? (*2 marks*)
5 What is meant by a partner's implied authority? (*2 marks*)
6 Give two reasons why joint and several liability is always accepted by partners in bank mandate forms? (*2 marks*)
7 When a partnership is dissolved, in what order should liabilities be met and from what sources? (*2 marks*)
8 If a partnership operates under a firm name, a bank should always open an account for it under that name. Why? (*2 marks*)
9 State the Rule in *Clayton's Case* (1816). (*2 marks*)
10 Why must cheques drawn by a partner after the commencement of his bankruptcy be confirmed by the other partners? (*2 marks*)

Answers on page 10

Topic 4   Companies

1 What basic principle of company law was established in *Salomon v. Salomon & Co.* (1897)? (*2 marks*)
2 What is the meaning of the words '*ultra vires*'? (*2 marks*)
3 Why is the decision in *Victors Ltd. v. Lingard* (1927) important to bankers? (*2 marks*)
4 State the Rule in *Turquand's Case* (1856). (*2 marks*)
5 Within how many days of its creation must a charge executed by a company be registered under the Companies Act 1985, s.395? (*2 marks*)
6 Why do banks insist on taking 'all moneys' debentures? (*2 marks*)
7 Distinguish between a fixed and a floating charge. (*2 marks*)
8 What is a 'Romalpa Clause' and what is the significance of such a clause to a banker? (*2 marks*)

9 What is meant by a 'preference'? (*2 marks*)
10 Name two preferential debts in the winding-up of a company. (*2 marks*)

Answers on page 12

Topic 5 Bankruptcy

1 Define a bankrupt. (*1 mark*)
2 List six acts of bankruptcy. (*3 marks*)
3 What are the effects of the making of a receiving order? (*2 marks*)
4 At what stage in the bankruptcy process does title to the debtor's property become vested in his trustee in bankruptcy? (*2 marks*)
5 Define a fraudulent preference. (*2 marks*)
6 Subject to three conditions, the Bankruptcy Act 1914 protects any payment of money or delivery of property to a person subsequently adjudicated bankrupt or a person claiming by assignment from him. What are these conditions? (*3 marks*)
7 What important example of preferential status available to a banker in a company's liquidation is not available in the bankruptcy process? (*2 marks*)
8 State and account for the action taken in regard to payments in when a banker has received notice of an act of bankruptcy committed by his customer. (*2 marks*)
9 To whom may payments be safely made in these same circumstances? (*2 marks*)
10 What protection is afforded to a banker if he pays a cheque to an undischarged bankrupt? (*2 marks*)

Answers on page 14

Topic 6 Land and its use as security

1 Distinguish between real and personal property. (*2 marks*)
2 Define and distinguish between an estate and an interest on land. (*2 marks*)
3 Why is it important to register a charge over unregistered land on the Land Charges Register? (*2 marks*)
4 What is an overriding interest under the Land Registration Act 1925? (*2 marks*)
5 Is the mortgagor the borrower or the lender? (*2 marks*)
6 Why is a legal mortgage to be preferred to an equitable mortgage? (*2 marks*)

7   Why must the mortgagor's account be broken when notice of a second mortgage is received by the first mortgagee? (*2 marks*)
8   How is a mortgage of registered land protected? (*2 marks*)
9   List the five remedies available to a legal mortgagee. (*2 marks*)
10 What is meant by the equity of redemption? (*2 marks*)

Answers on page 16

Topic 7   Life assurance policies and stocks and shares

1   Explain what is meant by an insurable interest. (*2 marks*)
2   Explain the principle of *uberrima fides* as applied to life policies. (*2 marks*)
3   What form does a banker's legal mortgage of a life policy take? (*2 marks*)
4   List the four rights of a legal mortgagee if the policy moneys have not become payable. (*2 marks*)
5   How is **a** a legal mortgage, and **b** an equitable mortgage of a life policy discharged? (*2 marks*)
6   How is title to registered securities transferred? (*2 marks*)
7   How do American and Canadian share certificates differ from other bearer securities? (*2 marks*)
8   How is an equitable mortgage of registered securities affected? (*2 marks*)
9   What is a blank transfer? (*2 marks*)
10 How is a mortgage of registered shares discharged? (*2 marks*)

Answers on page 17

Topic 8   Guarantees

1   Define a guarantee. (*2 marks*)
2   Distinguish between a guarantee and an indemnity. (*2 marks*)
3   Why should co-guarantors always assume joint and several liability in a bank guarantee? (*2 marks*)
4   Why must every co-guarantor sign the guarantee? (*2 marks*)
5   List the four main things done by a bank guarantee form. (*2 marks*)
6   Why does the surety guarantee the whole of the customer's indebtedness? (*2 marks*)
7   What is the purpose of the guarantor binding his personal representatves to the guarantee? (*2 marks*)
8   Why does a bank guarantee provide that the guarantor's liability arises on a written demand for repayment being made? (*2 marks*)

9 Explain the purpose of a bank guarantee form giving the bank the right to retain the guarantee form uncancelled for a minimum period of six months. (*2 marks*)

10 What is the effect of an *ultra vires* clause in a bank guarantee form? (*2 marks*)

Answers on page 19

Topic 9   Bills of exchange

1 Define a bill of exchange. (*2 marks*)
2 What are the legal characteristics of a bill of exchange? (*2 marks*)
3 What is meant by a fictitious or non-existing payee of a bill of exchange? (*1 mark*)
4 What is the effect of a forged indorsement on a bill? (*3 marks*)
5 Define a 'holder'. (*1 mark*)
6 Define a 'holder in due course'. (*3 marks*)
7 State the rights of a holder in due course. (*2 marks*)
8 What are the conditions for incurring liability on a bill of exchange? (*2 marks*)
9 How is a bill of exchange dishonoured? (*1 mark*)
10 List the ways in which a bill of exchange can be discharged. (*3 marks*)

Answers on page 21

Topic 10   Cheques

1 Define a cheque. (*1 mark*)
2 What is the legal status of a 'cheque' made out to cash? (*2 marks*)
3 What is the difference between a special and a general crossing on a cheque? (*2 marks*)
4 List five situations where banker's authority to pay a cheque is terminated. (*2 marks*)
5 What is the nature of a paying banker's possible liability in connection with a cheque? (*2 marks*)
6 What are the provisos in the protection given by the Bills of Exchange Act 1882, s.60? (*2 marks*)
7 What was the effect of the Cheques Act 1957, s.1? (*2 marks*)
8 When does the Cheques Act 1957, s.4 protect a banker? (*2 marks*)
9 List six different instances of possible negligence in the collection of cheques. (*3 marks*)

10 In what circumstances will a banker be the holder in due course of a cheque that he collects. (*2 marks*)

Answers on page 23

Answers

Topic 1 Banker and customer

1 a Keeping current accounts.
   b Paying cheques drawn on the bank
   c Collecting cheques for customers.
   These activities are stated in Paget's *Law of Banking* and were accepted by the Court of Appeal in *United Dominions Trust Ltd* v. *Kirkwood* (1966). (1 mark for each correct answer) /3

2 No, a person becomes a customer the moment an agreement (contract) is made to open an account in his or her name. /1

3 The contractual relationship of debtor and creditor. /2

4 *Bundy's Case* (1975) established that where a customer comes to trust and rely on a banker for advice, the banker can owe a very strict duty of good faith to the customer over and above the contractual obligations already owed. /2

5 *Macmillan & Arthur* (1918) established that a customer owes his banker a duty to draw cheques with reasonable care. /2

6 Set-off allows a banker to combine two or more accounts, thereby enabling him to reduce his liability to repay any credit balance by the amount of any debit balance. (1 mark for only mentioning combining accounts.) /2

7 The general exceptions are when:
   a He is compelled by law to do so.
   b He owes a duty to the public to do so.
   c His own interests require disclosure.
   d He has the express or implied consent of his customer to do so.
   (1 mark for each of two exceptions.) /2

8 He is the baillee. /2

9 *Hedley Byrne* (1963) established that a banker can be liable in tort for negligence for an incorrect opinion

or reference causing economic loss unless a suitable disclaimer was included in the statement. One mark for mentioning negligence, the second for mentioning the disclaimer.

Your score

/2

10 No.

/2

➤*your total score for this Topic* . . . . /20

Topic 2 The law of agency

1 An agent's main function is to make contracts on his principal's behalf. (1 mark for 'making contracts', 1 mark for 'on his principal's behalf'.)

/2

2 The distinction is to be found in the extent of their authority. A special agent is appointed to undertake a particular transaction and his authority is limited to that particular act (1 mark). A general agent has implied authority to act within the general course of his business (1 mark).

/2

3 **a** By contract; **b** by ratification; **c** by estoppel; **d** by operation of law. (1 mark for two correct, 2 marks for all four correct.)

/2

4 You should have selected from the following: **a** obediency; **b** care and skill; **c** personal performance; **d** good faith; **e** to account. (1 mark for two correct, 2 marks for all four correct.)

/2

5 No, unless he has reserved the right to keep the discount; this would be a breach of his duty of good faith: *Turnball v. Garden* (1869).

/2

6 Delegation is allowed where **a** express authority is given; **b** where implied authority exists, e.g. where a banker is asked to sell shares; **c** where the task delegated does not require the exercise of care and skill, e.g. signing documents; **d** where an unforeseen situation makes delegation necessary. (1 mark for two correct, 2 marks for all four).

/2

7 Clearly show that he is acting on behalf of somebody else, e.g. by signing 'per pro'.

/2

8 An agent is liable for any loss he causes by warranting (saying) he has authority when he hasn't. This is known as breach of warranty of authority.

/2

9

9 Agency may be irrevocable when it secures a personal interest of the agent, e.g. where the agent pays himself commission directly from the income he makes for the principal. Bank mortgage forms often contain an irrevocable power of attorney enabling the bank to transfer title to the mortgaged property on the mortgagor's behalf.

Your score

/2

10 You could have selected two from the following: **a** determining the extent of an agent's authority before dealing with him; **b** collecting cheques for customers; **c** borrowing by agents, particularly company directors; **d** agents signing bills of exchange. (1 mark for each example.)

/2

your total score for this Topic .... /20

Topic 3 Partnership

1 'Partnership is the relation which subsists between persons carrying on a business in common with a view of profit.' For 2 marks you must get the definition absolutely correct.

/2

2 A registered company has a separate legal identity, a partnership has not. This is a really basic point — if you got it wrong, you need to revise first principles of partnership and company law.

/2

3 The firm name is a partnership's business name and if it consists of anything other that the actual names of all the partners, the Business Names Act 1985 applies. For the first mark you must have stated that the names of all the partners must be legibly stated on all business letters and written demands for payment and give an address where court documents can be served and accepted. For the second mark you must have stated that the names and addresses of the partners must be displayed prominently in any place where business is carried on and to which customers have access.

/2

4 Primarily, a limited partner is one whose liability for the firm's debts is limited to the amount of his capital contribution. This is worth one mark. However, for the second mark, you should have stated that while he shares in the firm's profits, he does not participate in its management, nor is he an agent of the firm and his death, bankruptcy or mental disorder does not dissolve it.

Your score

/2

5 Implied authority (sometimes known as usual authority) is a partner's authority as it appears to others. Hence, he will always bind his fellow partners if he makes a contract in the usual course of his firm's business, irrespective of any actual internal limit on his authority, unless the other contracting party knew that he had no authority to enter the contract: Partnership Act 1890, s.5.

/2

6 No marks for explaining joint and several liability itself — you weren't asked to. Be careful!

You should have selected two reasons from the following four (1 mark for each).

a A credit balance on a partner's private account may be set-off against a debit balance on the firm account.

b The bank will rank equally with his separate creditors should a partner die or become bankrupt.

c Should the partnership itself become bankrupt, the bank will have a double right of proof, i.e. it may prove against both the joint estate of the firm and the separate estate of each partner.

d Security deposited by a partner for all personal liabilities may be appropriated by the bank against either his personal debt or the partnership debt.

/2

7 For one mark the order in which liabilities are settled is:

a Payment of outside creditors, according to the priority of their debts.

b Repayment of loans to the firm made by the partners.

c Repayment of each partner's capital contribution. Any remainder is divided among the partners according to their rights to share in the firm's profits.

For the second, payments should be made from, in order:

11

**Your
score**

a Undrawn profits.
b The firm's capital.
c The partners personally in the proportions in which they were entitled to share profits.

/2

8 By opening an account in the firm name, the bank is able to take action against all the partners, both known and unknown, should it need to.

/2

9 The Rule in *Clayton's Case* (1816) states that in a current account payments-in are appropriated to debit items in chronological order unless the customer or banker has taken steps to appropriate particular credits to particular debits.
   You really must know this! There are numerous examples of its importance in banking. For 2 marks your explanation must be exact, although, of course, a paraphrase of the one given is OK.

/2

10 Quite simply, because his bankruptcy terminates his authority as agent of the firm. Thus a banker who paid such a cheque would have no mandate to do so.

/2

your total score for this Topic . . . . /20

Topic 4 Companies

1 The case established that a registered company has a legal existence (personality) quite separate and distinct from its members. If you remember the case, you'll recall that Salomon lent money to 'his' company and was its only secured creditor. When the company went into liquidation, he was entitled to all the available assets as the only secured creditor, the unsecured creditors getting nothing at all. It was a situation where the principle established was more important than the claims heard, although the unsecured creditors probably didn't see it that way!

/2

2 These Latin words mean 'beyond the power of'. In company law they are used to describe a company's activities that are outside the scope of the objects clause in its memorandum of association or the actions of a director which exceed his authority. However, you score 2 marks if you accurately explained the meaning of the words alone.

/2

*Your
score*

3   The decision illustrates the problems associated with the passing of a resolution where one or more directors has a personal interest in it; 1 mark for this. For the second mark, you must have said that if the resolution was to give security to the bank, a bank's knowledge of the company's articles may prevent it relying on *Turquand's Case* if directors' personal interests are involved. This could mean the security becomes unenforceable. A difficult question to answer!

/2

4   The Rule states that a person dealing with a company is taken to know the contents of its memorandum and articles of association and he must ensure that the proposed transaction is consistent with them. However, he may assume that the company has properly completed any internal formalities which may be required before the transaction can be entered into by the company.

    1 mark if you made the point about 'knowing' the contents; a second mark for the 'assumption' that can be made.

/2

5   21 days.

/2

6   A bank always protects itself against all foreseeable eventualities. By taking an 'all moneys' debenture, it obtains a security which secures all moneys owing on any account at any time and one which will always keep pace with the overdrawn balance(s).

/2

7   A fixed charge is a legal or equitable mortgage of specified property. A floating charge is an equitable charge which floats over the fluctuating assets of a company, e.g. its stock, without attaching to specific assets until it crystallises, i.e. becomes fixed. 1 mark for each definition.

/2

8   A 'Romalpa clause' is a retention of title clause. Such a clause is often found in a contract for the supply of goods and provides that title to the goods does not pass until they've been paid for (1 mark for explaining this). A Romalpa clause poses a threat to any floating charge a banker may have taken over the buyer's goods. This is because some of the goods may still belong to a supplier and therefore not be

covered by the charge: the second mark for explaining this.

9 A preference under the Insolvency Act 1985, s.101(4) is where a company does anything which has the effect of putting a creditor or a guarantor for any of its debts or liabilities in a *better position* in the event of the company going into insolvent liquidation than he would have been in had that thing not been done. The company must have been unable to pay its debts at the time of the preference and have been influenced by a desire to improve the position of the person preferred. There are also time requirements that must be satisfied.

/2

10 You should have selected two from the following list (1 mark for each):
— VAT (6 months).
— Taxes (12 months).
— Wages and salaries.
— Holiday pay.
— Advances to make payments for wages/salaries or holiday pay.
— National Insurance contributions.

/2

➤ *your total score for this Topic* . . . . /20

Topic 5 Bankruptcy

1 A bankrupt is a person against whom an adjudication order has been made by the courts. Right or wrong. An apparently basic question to start with but many students who know a lot about bankruptcy can not answer it! Always learn your basic definitions.

/1

2 Altogether there are ten acts of bankruptcy — eight under the Bankruptcy Act 1914 and two added by later legislation. You score one mark for each of two acts you listed.
a An assignments for the benefit of creditors.
b A fraudulent conveyance.
c A fraudulent preference.
d Misconduct — deliberately avoiding creditors.
e Execution levied against the debtor's goods.
f Debtor's own action, i.e. filing a bankruptcy petition.

*Your
score*

g Non-compliance with a bankruptcy notice.
h Notice that he intends to suspend payment of his debts.
i The making of a criminal bankruptcy order.
j Revocation of an administration order.

/3

3 First, the receiving order makes the Official Receiver the receiver of the debtor's property; 1 mark for this. Second, and more importantly, it prevents the debtor from disposing of his property and prevents creditors proceeding individually against him; 1 mark for stating this. Remember that the receiving order does not make the debtor bankrupt nor take away his or her title to property.

/2

4 A straightforward question; the adjudication order vests title to the debtor's property in the trustee in bankruptcy. It also makes the debtor bankrupt.

/2

5 A fraudulent preference is the conveyance of property to, or charging property in favour of, a particular creditor, or any surety for a debt owed to that particular creditor, with the intention of giving him or the surety preference over other creditors.

Quite a complicated definition but it is important, not least because you're often set questions on the topic. Learn your definitions. You score 1 mark for the 'conveyance, transfer or charge' part and the second mark for the 'intention' part.

/2

6 The three conditions are that the transaction must take place:
   a Before the date of the receiving order.
   b Without notice of the presentation of a petition.
   c In the ordinary course of business or otherwise *bona fide*.
You score 1 mark for each correct condition, 3 marks in all.

/3

7 Under the Insolvency Act 1985, a person who advances money to pay wages, salaries and accrued holiday pay is a preferential creditor in a company's liquidation. It is this right that is (at present) unavailable in the bankruptcy process.

/2

8 Payments into the account must be held in a suspense account for three months (1 mark) in case a

petition is based upon the act and the payments claimed by the trustee (1 mark).

Your score /2

9 Payments may only be made to the debtor or to a person claiming by assignment from him, e.g. a trustee named in a deed of arrangement; for this, 1 mark. For the second mark you should have mentioned that even these payments can only be made if the account is in credit since debts contracted, e.g an overdraft, after notice of an available act of bankruptcy are not provable.

/2

10 The Bills of Exchange Act 1882, s.60, protects a banker if he pays a cheque to an undischarged bankrupt provided that the payment was in good faith and in the ordinary course of business.

/2

═══════▷*your total score for this Topic* . . . . /20

Topic 6 Land and its use as security

1 Freehold land is the only type of property classed as real property; personal property is everything else, including leasehold land. The distinction is a product of legal history.

/2

2 A more difficult question than it may at first seem since both estates and interests are abstract legal ideas quite separate from the land to which they relate. Basically, an estate is a right to the land itself (1 mark for this) while an interest in land is a right to a claim against the land of another less than actual possession (a second mark for explaining this).

/2

3 An unregistered charge is void against a purchaser for value. A mortgagee is a purchaser within the meaning of the act.

/2

4 An overriding interest is one which could be discovered from enquiries of the occupier or by an inspection of the land itself and not, if the land were unregistered, from the title deeds and documents relating to the land.

/2

5 The borrower; we trust that you didn't get this one wrong!

/2

6 An equitable mortgage gives the mortgagee

16

Your score

(personal) rights of action against the mortgagor to recover the debt (1 mark). A legal mortgage gives rights against the property mortgaged in addition to rights against the mortgagor personally (1 mark).

/2

7 The first point you should have made is that notice of a second mortgage terminates the bank's mortgage as a continuing security. Give yourself 1 mark if you explained this. For the second mark you must have explained that the account is broken to avoid the Rule in *Clayton's Case* (1816), working to the bank's disadvantage. You must know this rule in its various applications.

/2

8 Did you distinguish between legal and equitable mortgages? In both cases protection is by registration at the Land Registry (1 mark). A charge is registered in the case of a legal mortgage; a notice of deposit of a land certificate in the case of an equitable mortgage (1 mark).

/2

9 Score 1 mark for listing at least three, 2 marks for listing all five. The remedies are:
a An action for the debt.
b Sale of the property.
c Appointment of a receiver.
d Foreclosure.
e Taking possession of the property.

/2

10 The equity of redemption is the mortgagor's right to pay off the mortgage after the legal redemption date has passed.

/2

your total score for this Topic ..../20

Topic 7 Life assurance policies and stocks and shares

1 An insurable interest is essentially a pecuniary interest: the financial loss which would be suffered by the proposer on the death of the person whose life is insured — 1 mark for this. However, a person always has an insurable interest in his or her own life and in that of his or her spouse irrespective of any pecuniary interest — you score your second mark for stating this.

/2

2   *Uberrima fides* means 'utmost good faith'. In the context of life assurance policies it puts the proposer under a duty to dislose all material facts, and failure to do so means that the insurer can avoid the contract if he wishes. Score 1 mark for explaining what the words mean and a second mark for explaining their effect in a life assurance contract.

3   An assignment under seal.

4   If the policy moneys have not become payable, a legal mortgagee may:
    a   Surrender the policy to the company.
    b   Obtain a loan from the company against the policy.
    c   Sell the policy.
    d   Convert the policy into a paid-up policy for a smaller capital sum.
    Score one mark for each of two correct answers.

5   A legal mortgage is discharged by a reassignment under seal (1 mark) and an equitable mortgage by cancelling the memorandum of deposit that will have been taken and given to the issuing company if notice of the mortgage was originally sent to it (1 mark).

6   Title to registered securities is transferred by lodging the transfer form, signed by the transferor, and the relevant certificate with the issuing organization for appropriate entries to be made on the register. To score 2 marks, your answer must mention all aspects.

7   Title to them is registered.

8   An equitable mortgage of registered stocks and shares is affected by a deposit of the share certificates (1 mark). A memorandum of deposit is invariably taken as well (1 mark).

9   A blank transfer form is an incomplete stock transfer form. It will usually omit the date and the name of the transferor but will contain details of the securities concerned and the mortgagor's signature as transferor.

10   A legal mortgage is discharged by a re-transfer of

Your score

/2

/2

/2

/2

/2

/2

/2

/2

title to the shares from the bank, or its nominee
company, to the customer (1 mark). An equitable
mortgage is discharged by returning the share
certificates to the customer and cancelling the
memorandum of deposit (1 mark).

/2

━━▷*your total score for this Topic* ..../20

Topic 8   Guarantees

1   A guarantee is defined by the Statute of Frauds
1677, s.4 as a promise to answer 'for the debt,
default or miscarriage of another' if that person fails
to meet his obligation. To score your 2 marks you
don't have to have made a correct reference to the
Statute but you must have got the rest.

/2

2   The respective effects of a guarantee and an
indemnity are similar in that each provides for the
payment of a sum of money. However, for 1 mark
you should have said that under a guarantee only
secondary liability is incurred while under an
indemnity primary liability is incurred. For the
second mark you must have stated that a guarantee
must be evidenced in writing to be enforceable; this
is not so with an indemnity.

/2

3   Joint liability enables the bank to claim against any
one, or any combination of the co-guarantors
(1 mark). Several liability ensures that on the death
or bankruptcy of a co-guarantor his estate remains
liable on the guarantee (1 mark).

/2

4   If one of a number of co-guarantors does not sign
the guarantee, it cannot be enforced against the
others.

/2

5   A bank guarantee form will:
   a   State the liability of the surety.
   b   Detail the circumstances in which the guarantee
       can be determined.
   c   Exclude all of the guarantor's most important
       common law rights against both the bank and the
       principal debtor.

d Exclude the operation of the Rule in *Clayton's Case* (1816).
Score 1 mark for each of two correct answers.

Your score /2

6 The whole of the customer's indebtedness is guaranteed for two reasons (1 mark for each):
 a It prevents him claiming part of any security held by the bank unless he meets all the indebtedness.
 b It prevents the guarantor proving against the customer's estate in bankruptcy in competition with the bank.

/2

7 If personal representatives are bound by the guarantee, the guarantee automatically remains in force when and if the surety dies (1 mark) and removes the necessity to break the account to prevent the Rule in *Clayton's Case* (1816) operating to the bank's detriment (1 mark).

/2

8 The guarantor's liability is stated to arise on a written demand for repayment being made so that the six year limitation period under the Limitation Act 1980 commences when such a demand is made and not from the date of the guarantee.

/2

9 By giving the right to retain the guarantee uncancelled for a period of at least six months, the bank protects itself should the repayment by its customer amount to a fraudulent preference. If this was so, the customer's trustee in bankruptcy could recover the repayment from the bank if it was made within the six months immediately preceding the presentation of the bankruptcy petition. Meanwhile, the bank would have released the security it held for the debt and would be left with only the right to prove in its customer's bankruptcy.

/2

10 The inclusion of an *ultra vires* clause in a guarantee has the effect of making the guarantee an indemnity should the principal debt prove to be unenforceable, for example where a loan was made to a company for what turns out to be an *ultra vires* purpose.

/2

➡️ *your total score for this Topic* . . . . /20

Topic 9   Bills of exchange

1   A bill of exchange is defined by the Bills of Exchange Act 1882, s.3(1) as '. . . an unconditional order in writing, addressed by one person to another, signed by the person giving it, requiring the person to whom it is addressed to pay on demand or at a fixed or determinable future time a sum certain in ·money to or to the order of a specified person, or to bearer.'

Quite a long definition which you may well not have got word perfect. For 2 marks you must have all the important points, for 1 mark, one omission.   /2

2   Different books list the characteristics in different ways but there are four you should have identified. Score 1 mark for each two you got right.

a   Title is transferable by delivery or, in the case of instruments payable to order, by indorsement completed by delivery.

b   A person taking the transfer in good faith and for value is not affected by any defects in the title of the transferor; he is said to take the instrument 'free from equities'.

c   The holder can sue in his own name.

d   The holder need not give notice to prior parties to establish his title.   /2

3   First of all, the expressions don't mean someone that doesn't actually exist; Father Christmas, for example (or perhaps he does?). Cases show that a fictitious or non-existing payee is a person to whom the drawer never intended to make payment.   /1

4   By s.24 of the 1882 Act, a forged or unauthorized signature is 'wholly inoperative'. This means that such signatures are not signatures at all. Score 1 mark if you made this point. The specific effects are that (i) the payee or indorser whose signature it appears to be incurs no liability on the bill, and (ii) on an order bill it fails to transfer title. Score 1 mark for each of these points.   /3

5   A holder is defined by s.2 as 'the payee or indorsee of a bill who is in possession of it, or the bearer of a

bearer bill'. For your mark you must have the definition correct in substance with only minor errors in the actual words.

6   A holder in due course is defined by s.29(1). We're altering the Act's layout and wording of the definition so that we can highlight the points you should have made. Here goes:

A holder in due course is a '... holder who has taken a bill:

a   Complete and regular on the face of it.

b   Before it was overdue.

c   Without notice that it had been previously dishonoured (if in fact it had).

d   In good faith.

e   For value.

f   Without notice of any defect in the title of the person who negotiated it.'

You can see that we've identified six key things in the definition; score 1 mark for each two you identified.

/3

7   The rights of a holder in due course are to:

a   Sue any prior party to the bill in his own name.

b   Take the bill free from equities.

c   Transfer his title as holder in due course to any person for value or as a gift, provided that that person was not a party to any defect which affected the bill.

For 2 marks you must have all three, 1 mark for two.

/2

8   There are four conditions which must be satisfied in order to incur liability on a bill of exchange; a person must:

a   Sign it.

b   Deliver it.

c   Possess contractual capacity.

d   Receive consideration.

Score 1 mark for each two conditions you listed.

/2

9   An easy question; a bill of exchange can be dishonoured by **a** non-acceptance or **b** non-payment. No half-marks.

/1

10 A bill of exchange can be discharged in five ways: *Your score*
   a By payment in due course.
   b By merger.
   c By renunciation.
   d By cancellation.
   e By material alteration.
   1 mark for two ways, 2 marks for four and 3 marks
   if you stated all five.   /3

➤*your total score for this Topic* ..../20

Topic 10 Cheques

1 A cheque is a bill of exchange drawn on a banker
   payable on demand: Bills of Exchange Act
   1882, s.73.   /1

2 A 'cheque' made out to cash is not a cheque at all
   since it is not made payable to anybody — 1 mark for
   this. However, it is a valid order to the bank from the
   customer to pay the stated amount from his or her
   account — the second mark for explaining this.   /2

3 A special crossing instructs payment to be made to a
   particular bank (1 mark), a general crossing enables a
   cheque to be paid through any bank account
   (1 mark).   /2

4 Five situations in which a banker's authority to pay a
   cheque is terminated are:
   a Countermand.
   b Issue of a garnishee order.
   c Notice of the customer's death.
   d Notice of a bankruptcy petition against the
     customer.
   e Notice of a winding-up order against the
     customer.
   Give yourself 1 mark for three correct examples,
   2 marks for all five.   /2

5 A paying banker can incur liability by:
   a Wrongfully debiting an account.
   b Wrongfully dishonouring a cheque.
   1 mark for each.   /2

6 The provisos in s.60 are that payment must be made:

a   In good faith.
b   In the ordinary course of business.
    Again, 1 mark for each point.   /2

7   The Cheques Act 1957, s.1 removed the need for
    cheques paid straight into the payee's account to be
    indorsed.   /2

8   The Cheques Act 1957, s.4 protects a collecting
    banker when he collects a cheque:
    a   For a customer.
    b   In good faith.
    c   Without negligence.
        1 mark for two points, 2 marks for all three points.   /2

9   Six possible instances of negligence in the collection
    of cheques are:
    a   Failure to ask for references.
    b   Failure to check references.
    c   Failure to obtain details of a customer's
        employer.
    d   Collecting cheques payable to a company for the
        account of an employee.
    e   Collecting cheques drawn by an agent on his
        principal's account for the agent's private
        account.
    f   Collecting 'Account payee' cheques for someone
        other than the named payee.
        1 mark for each two correct answers.   /3

10 A collecting banker will be the holder in due course
    of a cheque when he himself gives value for it,
    e.g. cashing a cheque drawn on another branch.   /2

your total score for this Topic . . . . /20

When you have completed all the short answer tests, fill in your
score grid (inside the back cover). You can now use your results
in this section to rank your revision priorities, starting with your
weakest topic first.

Topics

For each topic, start with the study guide and then answer the multiple choice questions which follow.

Topic 1 Banker and customer

Study guide

You'll probably already know that the Institute's examination does not include any specific questions on the banker–customer relationship. However, this is far more than an introductory chapter for the simple reason that the law covered by the syllabus is about people and the services banks provide to them, i.e. the transactions between banks and their customers. We must start with two definitions.

Definitions

Banker Acts of Parliament are not really helpful for our purposes here since they talk about banks and bankers as institutions or about the regulations which govern them. You need to define a banker in terms of what he does.

The best functional definition is probably that of the Court of Appeal in *United Dominions Trust Ltd v. Kirkwood* (1966), where the performance of the following *three activities* were identified as the characteristics of a banker.

1 Accepting money from and collecting cheques for their customers and placing them to their credit.
2 Honouring cheques or orders drawn on them by their customers and debiting their customers accordingly.
3 Keeping current accounts in which the credits and debits are entered.

You don't need to learn this definition by heart but you must be familiar with it.

Customer This definition is more important to you because there are instances, e.g. under the Bills of Exchange Act 1882, where the legal position is dependent upon whether or not the banker *acted for a customer*. You should learn the following simple definition.

A customer of a bank is a person who has entered into a contract with a banker for the opening of an account in his name.

Remember that *Ladbroke v. Todd* (1914) established that a person becomes a customer as soon as the bank accepts him or her as a customer; no course of dealings is required.

The banker–customer relationship

Having noted our two basic definitions, we can move onto the banker–customer relationship. Remember the following two basic points.

1 It is basically the *contractual relationship of debtor and creditor.* (When the account is in credit, the bank is the debtor and when overdrawn, the creditor.)
2 Three acts of rules regulate the relationship.
   a *Contract law.* The exam will not contain questions on contract law as such and you are unlikely to gain anything revising the whole subject at this stage.
   b The rules of *agency and bailment.* The former we will look at in detail in the *Topic Guide* on Agency. You should know the following about the latter:
      — The definition of bailment.
      — The legal distinction between a gratuitous (unpaid) bailee and a bailee for reward (paid).
      — How the rules apply to safe custody arrangements.
      Bailment is, however, an unlikely question.
   c *Banking practice.* You will have seen many examples of this during your studies and how it becomes incorporated into the law through court decisions. The many cases on s.4 of the Cheques Act 1957 are good examples of this process.

Before we leave this topic, remember that the Court of Appeal in *Lloyds Bank v. Bundy* (1975) — the case about the elderly farmer who mortgaged his house to secure his son's business overdraft — added a new dimension to the relationship. Essentially, a bank can find itself, quite independent of the contractual relationship, owing a very strict duty of good faith to its customer when he or she has come to *trust* and *rely* on the bank for advice.

Specific aspects of the banker–customer relationship

1 *Safe custody arrangements* You've already seen that this involves the rules of bailment. In most cases a bank can be regarded as a bailee for reward, whether or not a special payment is made, since a safe custody

facility is usually considered part of the wider contractual relationship. In practice the point is largely academic in normal branch banking since the same standard of care is taken of all safe custody deposits whether paid for or not.

2 *Opinions and references* Assuming a banker would never deliberately make a false statement — in which case he would incur liability in tort for deceit — you're concerned with the possibility of the statement being made negligently. Here you should know the case of *Hedley Byrne & Co v. Heller Partners Ltd* (1963), a decision which was of considerable importance in the development of the general law on negligence.

3 *Bank statements* Remember, while the bank owes a duty to provide statements, the customer does not owe a duty to check them. This means that the customer can subsequently challenge their accuracy. It's worth knowing the case of *United Overseas Bank v. Jiwani* (1976), which governs the bank's ability to recover excess credits (we cover this later on).

A banker's rights and duties

Virtually all textbooks dealing with the subject will give you lists of rights and duties and they will not be identical. This does not mean one is right and the others wrong; it's a matter of grouping and phrasing. If you haven't a convenient list of the rights and duties either in your notes or in a textbook, you could usefully make one. Keep the notes brief; remember our advice in the *Editor's Introduction*.

Once again, the list is something to be understood rather than learnt at this point. It's far better to learn the important ones in their wider context at the appropriate time, for example, a banker's right to a lien over securities, reliance on the rule in *London Joint Stock Bank v. Macmillan & Arthur* (1918), and the provisos to the duty to honour customer's cheques. Of course, if any of these are unfamiliar to you, you should remedy this now!

Once you feel confident about your knowledge of this topic, try to answer the 10 multiple choice questions which follow.

Multiple choice questions

(Note that, since this first chapter is an introductory one covering a wide assortment of topics, some of which we will look at in greater detail later, the MCQs are also wide ranging. Don't worry if you find some rather difficult at this stage. Remember, you won't have to answer questions on the banker-customer relationship specifically.)

1   Which of the following is not an accepted criterion for determining status as a banker:

   a   keeping current accounts?
   b   offering loan and overdraft facilities?
   c   paying cheques drawn on the bank?
   d   collecting cheques for his customers?

 *answer*

2   Which of the following is essential to establishing a person as a customer of a bank:

   a   cashing cheques for that person?
   b   a course of dealing between that person and the bank?
   c   opening an account in the person's name?
   d   agreeing to open an account in the person's name?

 *answer*

3   Which of the following is not central to the legal framework regulating the banker–customer relationship:

   a   the law of contract?
   b   the law of tort?
   c   the law of agency?
   d   banking practice?

 *answer*

4   *Lloyds Bank v. Bundy* (1975), established that:

   a   a banker owes only a contractual duty of care to his customers.
   b   a banker can owe a customer a duty of care over and above that

imposed by the contract between them.

c   a banker owes a fiduciary duty to all his customers.

d   a banker can owe a fiduciary duty to certain of his customers.

5   A banker's lien:

a   entitles a banker to retain possession of all a customer's securities and other property which may be deposited with the bank as security for any money owed to the bank.

b   entitles a banker to demand that further securities be deposited to cover any borrowing in excess of the agreed figure.

c   is lost when the bank relinquishes possession of the securities, even temporarily.

d   entitles a banker to sell the securities covered by the lien.

6   *London Joint Stock Bank v. Macmillan & Arthur* (1918) established that:

a   a customer owes a duty to his banker to complete a bill of exchange drawn on the bank with reasonable care.

b   a customer owes a duty to his banker to draw a cheque with reasonable care.

c   an acceptor of a bill of exchange is not under a duty to take precautions against the bill's subsequent alteration.

d   a customer can in certain circumstances be estopped (prevented) from denying the genuiness of a forged signature on a cheque.

7   In which of the following situations is a banker still under a duty to pay his customer's cheques:

a   when a garnishee order has been made against the bank?

b   when the bank has had notice of an act of bankruptcy by the customer?

c   when the bank has received a telephone countermand of a cheque?

d when the bank has received notice of the customer's death?

answer

8 Under a 'night safe' arrangement, the bank:

  a becomes a gratuitous bailee.
  b becomes a bailee for reward.
  c obtains a lien over the deposits for any monies owed to the bank.
  d becomes the owner of the deposits.

answer

9 When a banker gives an inaccurate opinion or reference about a customer:

  a he may be liable to his customer for breach of contract.
  b he may be liable to the party requesting the opinion or reference for breach of contract.
  c he may be liable in tort.
  d he can invariably exclude all possible liability by including a suitable disclaimer.

answer

10 If a banker over-credits a customer's account, the customer:

  a is under a duty to repay the amount over-credited.
  b can always keep the money because he does not owe a duty to check the accuracy of his bank statements.
  c cannot be made to repay the over-credit if he has already spent it.
  d may keep the money in certain circumstances.

answer

Answers follow on pages 32-35. Score 2 marks for each correct answer.

Answers

1 The correct answer is **b**.

Loan and overdraft facilities (answer **b**) are both extremely common in ordinary branch banking so you can be forgiven for thinking that they are necessarily part of a banker's activities. However, the other three functions are far more fundamental. All three are provided to all current account customers and they received judicial recognition in *United Dominions Trust Ltd. v. Kirkwood* (1966).

2 The correct answer is **d**.

A contract is the basis of the banker–customer relationship and once an agreement has been reached to open an account — all the forms filled in and accepted, references taken etc. — the required contract has been made. It follows that answer **c** — actually opening the account — is something which is done once the contractual relationship has actually been established. The same applies to answer **a** — cashing cheques. Remember too that on payment of a fee and production of your cheque card, a bank will normally cash a cheque for you even if you are definitely not its customer. Answer **b** is wrong because it was expressly established in *Ladbroke v. Todd* (1914) that a course of dealings is not essential to establish the banker–customer relationship.

3 The correct answer is **b**.

While it is true that the law of tort is important in certain aspects of banking, e.g. negligence when giving opinions or paying cheques, the legal framework of the relationship is basically an amalgam of contract and agency law and the rules of established banking practice.

4 The correct answer is **b**.

Bundy's Case (1975) established that when a customer comes to trust and rely on a bank for advice, the bank can owe that customer a very strict duty of good faith. If you remember, in the actual case the bank's own interest conflicted with that of its customer and it broke its duty of good faith by not ensuring that its customer received independent professional advice before mortgaging his home for a second time. Since answer **b** is right, answer **a** must be wrong. Of more interest are answers **c** and **d**. The duty established in *Bundy's Case* is very similar in concept and for all banking purposes as onerous as a fiduciary duty which, as you may remember, is a creation of Equity — the rules originally developed and applied in the old Court of Chancery. However, there is a closed list of relationships which automatically create a fiduciary duty, e.g. parent–child, solicitor–client. The banker–customer relationship is specifically not one of them. The unusual facts of *Bundy's Case* were held to give rise to a special relationship.

5 The correct answer is **c**.

A lien is a right to retain possession of the property of another until payment of a debt from that person has been made. In other words, possession is retained in lieu of payment. Thus, if a bank relinquishes possession, even temporarily, the lien is lost. Answer **a** is incorrect because this could include a safe custody deposit. Such a deposit is not intended ever to be used for security purposes. To be absolutely certain about the position, it is usual practice for a memorandum of deposit to be signed. This specifically states that the property deposited is deposited as security and not for safe custody. Answer **b** is incorrect because while the effect of the lien is that the customer may deposit further securities to release the property covered by it, a banker cannot demand this. In some cases a banker's lien does entitle the banker to sell the securities covered by the lien, e.g. a lien over a bill of lading gives the right of sale over the goods that the bill represents, but this is not invariably the case with other securities. So answer **d** is not absolutely correct.

6 The correct answer is **b**.

It's perfectly true that a customer may be estopped from denying the genuiness of a forged signature on a cheque but this was established in such cases as *Greenwood* v. *Martins Bank* (1933) and not in *Macmillan & Arthur*. Likewise, answer **c** is a true statement of the law but was established in *Schofield v. Earl of Londesbrough* (1896). If you remember, in *Macmillan & Arthur* the defendant's clerk made out a cheque in figures only and had it signed by his employees. He then fraudulently altered the figures and filled in the words to match the amount as altered. The decision specifically applies to cheques, not bills of exchange generally; so, while a cheque is a bill of exchange drawn on a banker — Bills of Exchange Act 1882, s.73 — answer **a** is imprecise.

7 The correct answer is **b**.

A garnishee order (answer **a**) is a court order to a banker ordering him not to pay money out of a customer's account(s) and so must relieve a banker of his duty to pay that customer's cheques. Notice of his customer's death (answer **d**) also terminates his mandate to pay. Answer c (a telephone countermand) is perhaps a little debateable because only the receipt of a written countermand is an effective 'stop' on the cheque. However, it is usual to delay payment of a cheque after receiving a telephone countermand pending the receipt of written confirmation. Perhaps somewhat surprisingly, notice of an act of bankruptcy (answer **b** has no effect on the operation of the account. However, it obviously puts a banker on the alert because the presentation of a bankruptcy petition, whether or not he has notice of it, does end his duty to pay cheques drawn by the customer.

8   The correct answer is **a**.

Answer **a** is correct simply because the usual night safe agreement will specify that this should be so. Answer **b** (bailee for reward) must necessarily be wrong therefore. You already know from question 5 that safe custody deposits are excluded from the scope of a banker's lien so answer **c** cannot be correct. You should also be able to remember that while possession transfers from a bailor to a bailee under a contract of bailment, ownership stays with the bailor; so, answer **d** is incorrect.

9   The correct answer is **c**.

A banker owes a duty of secrecy to his customer concerning his affairs but it's well established that a banker has implied permission to answer a status enquiry from a third party unless instructed not to do so. Answer **a** is therefore incorrect. Answer **b** is wrong because the opinion or reference would not be given under a contract; no payment or other consideration would be given. Liability in tort, the correct answer, could be of two kinds. Firstly, liability for deceit if the inaccuracy was deliberate — an almost inconceivable situation — and secondly liability for negligence under the principle established in *Hedley Byrne & Co. v. Heller Partners Ltd* (1963). Answer **d** (the use of disclaimers) raises an interesting point. The actual decision in *Hedley Byrne* was that the bank was protected by the pre-printed disclaimer on the opinion. However, the Unfair Contract Terms Act 1977 subjects such disclaimers to a test of 'reasonableness' and it is open to an aggrieved party in such a situation to challenge the validity of a particular disclaimer. So, including the word 'invariably' means that answer **d** is wrong; excluding the word would mean that it was right.

10   The correct answer is **d**.

Answers **b** and **c** are surely every customer's dream but they are both wrong — unfortunately! It's perfectly true that a customer owes no duty to check his bank statements (answer **b**) but it does not follow that he can keep any over-credit for this reason. Answer **c** (spending the money) could be pleaded as a reason for not making repayment but the customer's argument would clearly be destroyed if he knew his account had been over-credited in the first place! That leaves answers **a** and **d**. Answer **a** is incorrect for two reasons: first, the mistake is the bank's after all and, second, the customer might quite legitimately think his balance is correct and act accordingly. If, in so doing, he altered his position — through the bank's mistake remember — it might be grossly unfair to make him repay the money. This leads nicely onto the correct answer — **d**. In *United Overseas Bank v. Jiwani* (1976) it was held that a customer may defeat the bank's claim for repayment if **i** the bank misrepresented the state of the account; **ii** the customer was misled by the misrepresentation; and **iii** as a result the customer changed his position in a way which would make it unfair to require him to repay the money. Fortunately, such situations don't occur very often and diplomacy rather than the law is the preferred solution!

Score 2 marks for each correct answer. What was your score for this topic? Fill it in on the score grid.

If you scored 12 or less and are still a bit shaky on some points go back and look at the study guide again, before proceeding any further.

If you are sure you really understand and are familiar with the topic now, try the 10 further questions which are on pages 170-172.

Alternatively you can go on to the next topic and do all the post-tests together at the end.

Topic 2 The law of agency

Study guide

The general law

The modern commercial world could not function without agents. Increasing commercial complexity, specialization and pressure of time mean that businessmen frequently have to employ agents to effect their business for them. Banks both act as agents, e.g. collecting cheques for customers, and deal with agents, e.g. partners in a firm, directors of a company and, sometimes, persons holding power of attorney. So, one way and another agency is very important to the business of banking. The examination, however, only rarely has questions solely on agency. Usually there is a question combining agency and partnership (an application of the general law) or a question on agency as it specifically relates to banking.

It's always useful to be able to write out a simple *definition* of the subject you're studying. So, who is an agent?

> An *agent* is a person who acts on another's behalf, the other person being known as his *principal*.

Easy, but it's worth remembering. It's also the key to understanding the subject. For example, it explains why an agent generally incurs no liability on the contracts he makes — they are not his but his principal's. The law is very much concerned with the extent of this power to act on the principal's behalf and the liabilities the principal incurs as a consequence. We therefore have to consider both the external relationship of the principal and agent with third parties and the internal relationship between principal and agent.

Remember that anyone legally able to enter a particular contract can employ an agent to do so for him. Indeed, the agent need not himself have the necessary *contractual capacity*, e.g. a minor, but employing an agent with full capacity does not make up for the principal's own lack of capacity, e.g. an *ultra vires* act of a company.

Hopefully, these general points should put the subject in perspective. Structure your revisions of the general law around the following areas, taking each one in turn.

1 The difference between a *special* and a *general agent*.

2   The four ways *agency can be created.*

3   *Power of attorney.*

4   An agent's *duties* (about five are usually given in most books).

5   An agent's *rights* (perhaps three main ones).

6   Relations with *third parties.*

   a   Where the agent discloses his agency, the agent drops out of the transaction immediately and generally incurs neither rights nor liabilities on the contract.

   b   The doctrine of the undisclosed principal, as in *Keighley Maxstead v. Durant & Co.* (1901).

7   *Breach of warranty of authority*: many students misunderstand the principle established in *Collen v. Wright* (1856). If an agent acts without authority he is liable to the third party for any loss caused to him. However, liability is *not* under the contract he makes but for his warranty (assertion) that he had the authority which he had not. Indeed, it makes no difference if the agent was unaware he had no authority, for example, if he acts in ignorance of his principal's death, or relying on a forged power of attorney, as in *Starkey v. Bank of England* (1903).

8   *Termination* of agency.

   a   By performance.

   b   By act of the parties. Sometimes an agency agreement is irrevocable because revocation could cause the agent loss. For example, in a mortgage form the bank may be given irrevocable power of attorney to transfer title to the mortgaged property on the mortgagor's behalf. This enables the bank to realise the security far more easily if repayment is not made.

   c   By operation of law, e.g. the bankruptcy or liquidation of the principal.

Banking and agency

Quite apart from examination considerations, a good understanding of how the general law applies to banking is part of your professional knowledge. Remember, banks act as agents for their customers and deal with people who are themselves agents.

If an *agent operates an account* for his principal, the agent is a special agent. You must keep to the mandate and ensure that he does not exceed his authority. For example, an agent's authority to draw, accept and indorse cheques does not imply authority to negotiate overdraft

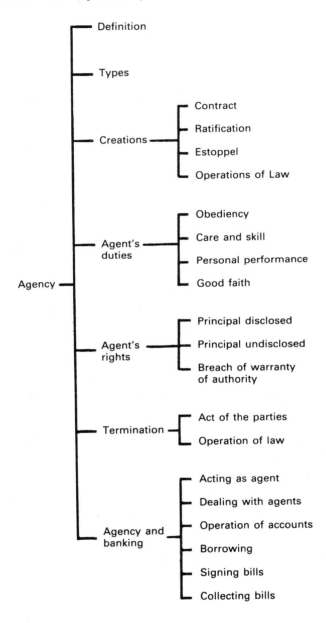

Fig. 2.1 *Revision diagram: Agency*

facilities or give or withdraw security.

Borrowing by an agent is another important area, particularly by a director on behalf of his company. Be sure you know and understand the *ultra vires* rule in relation to such borrowing. (We'll be covering this in detail in the *Topic: Companies.*)

Finally, agency and *bills of exchange*; remember:

a   When *signing a bill of exchange*, an agent will incur personal liability unless he clearly indicates that he acts on his principal's behalf, e.g. by a 'per pro' signature: Bills of Exchange Act 1882, s.26.

b   An obvious point, perhaps, but when a banker *collects a cheque as agent* for his customer, he must exercise care to follow normal banking practice.

c   When *collecting cheques for known agents* a banker must ensure that the agent is entitled to the money or lose the protection of the Cheques Act 1957, s.4. For example, drawing a cheque on his principal's account payable to himself! Remember *Midland Bank Ltd. v. Reckitt* (1933) and *Marquess of Bute v. Barclays Bank Ltd* (1955).

Before you answer the multiple-choice questions, spend some time working through the revision diagram of 'Agency' (Fig. 2.1).

Once you feel confident about your knowledge of this topic, try to answer the 10 multiple choice questions which follow.

Multiple choice questions

1 When an agent discloses his principal and, acting within his authority, makes a contract on his behalf:

   a   only the principal is liable on the contract.
   b   only the agent is liable.
   c   both principal and agent are liable.
   d   the other party can choose whom to hold liable on the contract.

2 The principal can ratify the contract where:

   a   the directors of a company, acting in good faith, enter into a contract which is outside the company's powers but which the company wishes to adopt?
   b   the agent expressly states he acts as agent but does not disclose who his principal is?
   c   before X Ltd was incorporated, a person who subsequently became its managing director entered into contracts on X Ltd's behalf for the supply of raw materials; one supplier refuses to fulfil his contract and denies that he is liable to X Ltd for breach of contract?
   d   the agent deliberately misled the other party into thinking that his principal had given him the authority to act as he did?

3 Agency by estoppel arises:

   a   from an existing contract between the principal and agent.
   b   through a rule of law.
   c   because of what the principal says or does.
   d   because of what the agent says or does.

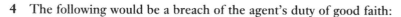

4 The following would be a breach of the agent's duty of good faith:

   a delegating his task to another.
   b using information he acquires during his work for his own purposes.
   c acting negligently.
   d not carrying out his task at all.

5 When an agent makes a contract without disclosing his agency, the third party may enforce the contract against:

   a the agent only.
   b the principal only.
   c the agent or the principal.
   d the agent and the principal.

6 An agent is liable for breach of warranty of authority:

   a under the contract he made with the third party.
   b even if he did not know that he had no authority.
   c even if he exceeded his authority through following his principal's ambiguous instructions.
   d even if the third party knows that he exceeded his authority.

7 Which of the following events does not end an agent's authority:

   a the death of the principal?
   b the mental disorder of the agent?
   c the bankruptcy of the principal?
   d the bankruptcy of the agent?

8 The principal can terminate the agency unless:

    a the agency was created by deed.

    b the agent is his employee.

    c the agency was granted as security for a debt owed by the principal to the agent.

    d he fails to tell previous clients that the agency has been ended.

9 If a director as agent of a company negotiates a loan which is *ultra vires* the company, a banker can:

    a rely on the company ratifying the transaction.

    b rely on the Companies Act 1985, s.35.

    c enforce the loan against the directors.

    d be subrogated to the rights of certain of the company's creditors.

10 In which of the following situations would a banker be acting in the normal course of business:

    a agreeing with an agent an overdraft facility on his principal's current account with authority to draw cheques on that account?

    b allowing an agent to draw cheques on a joint current account when only one party has authorized the agent to draw cheques?

    c collecting cheques for the account of X which were drawn payable to Y's principal and indorsed to X by Y?

    d collecting cheques for an agent drawn by the agent on his principal's account?

Answers follow on pages 43-47. Score 2 marks for each correct answer.

Answers

1 The correct answer is **a**.

No apologies for starting with such an easy question; it's important that you have the basic principles clear in your mind. The agent here is merely acting as the go-between. Answer **b** would be right only if the agent had acted without authority and the principal had chosen not to ratify (confirm and adopt) the contract.

Answers **c** and **d** apply to the situation where the agent does not disclose his agency but the principal ratifies the contract. Here both can be liable and the other contracting party can choose which to enforce the contract against.

2 The correct answer is **d**.

You know from the previous answer that ratification is where the principal confirms and adopts a contract entered into on his behalf by a person who had no authority to act for him when he made the contract.

Answer **a** is incorrect because the transaction is a legal nullity; technically it is *ultra vires* the objects clause. It's logically impossible to confirm and adopt something which does not exist. Do you remember the leading case of *Ashbury Railway Carriage Co v. Riche* (1875)? However, also remember the effect of the Companies Act 1985, s.35 (formerly the European Communities Act 1972, s.9(1)) on the other party's position.

If you think about answer **d**, there was legally something to adopt, albeit a contract voidable for misrepresentation. A contract which is voidable can be ratified before the other party exercises his right to rescind it (set it aside).

In answer **b**, ratification may not even be relevant because it doesn't state that the agent had exceeded his authority. If it did, it is well established that an undisclosed principal cannot ratify: *Keighley Maxstead v. Durant & Co* (1901).

Finally, answer **c** is wrong because the principal must be legally capable of making the contract both when the agent supposedly acted for him and when he ratified. A company yet to be incorporated doesn't exist at law and so is legally incapable of any act. So, the supplier is not liable to X Ltd. The contract is the agent's and he could both sue and be sued on it: Companies Act 1985, s.36 (formerly the European Communities Act 1972, s.9(2)).

3 The correct answer is **c**

Estoppel is a rule of evidence that prevents a person denying his previous acts or statements. Agency by estoppel arises where a principal allows a person to appear to be his agent to the outside world (answer **c**).

If you chose answer **a** (an existing contract) you're possibly confusing agency by estoppel with an agent's implied authority. For example, if a customer asks his banker to sell shares for him, the banker has implied authority to engage a broker to undertake the sale.

If agency by estoppel arose through a rule of law (answer **b**) it would mean that estoppel would apply in certain well defined situations. However, while certain general principles (which you should know) apply, each case depends on its own facts.

Answer **d** could possibly be a situation in which ratification might occur but estoppel certainly would not.

4 The correct answer is **b**.

An agent's duty of good faith is very strict. Clearly, it includes not accepting financial inducements from the third party and not disclosing confidential information about his principal. However, it also includes not using information he acquires during his agency for his own purposes, even if he acts in complete good faith; *Boardman v. Phipps* (1967) is a case in point.

The other three answers may constitute a breach of other duties but are not breaches of the duty of good faith. In particular, acting negligently is not acting in bad faith. Answer **a** may not even be a breach of any duty because in certain circumstances an agent may delegate his task. Look these up if you can't remember them.

5 The correct answer is **c**.

The correct answer basically owes more to commonsense than to the law. The contract was made on behalf of the principal but the third party thought he was dealing with the agent alone. Commonsense tells us that he should have the choice of enforcing the contract against whichever he likes. This excludes answers **a** and **b**.

Answer **d** is wrong because this would allow the third party to have his cake and eat it, so to speak. However, the law does allow the cake to be tasted, in a way, because starting an action against the agent does not prevent the third party changing his mind and deciding to sue the principal, or vice versa. Nevertheless, conclusive evidence of an election (as it is known), e.g. obtaining judgment, even if unsatisfied, bars subsequent action against the other.

6 The correct answer is **b**.

The decision in *Collen v. Wright* (1856), which established the rule, is designed to protect the third party, not the agent. At law it's sometimes a question of which of two innocent parties should be the one to suffer. So, even if the principal has died or become insane and the agent had no reasonable way of finding out, he is liable. A case relevant to bankers is *Starkey v. Bank of England* (1903), involving a forged power of attorney.

Providing the agent acted in good faith, the ambiguity of the instruction (answer **c**) absolves him and, clearly, the third party cannot sue the agent if he knew (answer **d**) that he didn't have the authority he professed; the third party cannot claim to have been misled.

Answer **a** is a common mistake students make. It can't be right, either because no contract is created — the agent has no authority to make it — or because the principal ratifies the contract thereby making it his own.

7 The correct answer is **d**.

However, while answer **d** is technically correct, it's highly likely that the principal would wish to end the relationship if this happened. On the face of it, it doesn't say much for the agent's own business abilities! If the agent's insolvency affected his fitness or ability to act as agent then the principal could undoubtedly terminate the agreement. The three other events all automatically terminate the principal–agent relationship. Remember, breach of warranty of authority (*Collen v. Wright* (1856)) is a possibility in relation to answers **a** and **c**.

8 The correct answer is **c**.

The reasoning behind this example is simply that it could cause the agent personal loss. An agency created by deed, i.e. a power of attorney (answer **a**), is no different to an agency created in any other way, except if it is expressed to be irrevocable. Hence, unless it is so expressed, or answer **c** or a similar example also applies, answer **a** is not correct. Nevertheless, if the revocation is unjustified, it will amount to a breach of contract entitling the agent to bring an action for the loss he suffers.

The fact that an agent is the principal's employee means that the agent would have the framework of employment law to protect him but this would not prevent the principal from actually terminating the agency, it would only give the agent rights and remedies if he did.

Answer **d** raises an important point. Previous clients are entitled to assume that the agency continues until they have evidence to the contrary from the principal. In other words, the principal may be estopped from denying that the agent continues to have his authority. Two points here; first, the operative word is 'may': each case depends on its facts. Second, we're talking about 'agency', i.e. one person's ability to enter into contracts which bind another person on whose behalf he acts. This may continue through estoppel even though the personal contractual relationship between the principal and agent has been ended.

9 The correct answer is **d**.

Let's start with answer **a**. This cannot be correct because a legal nullity — which this contract of loan is — cannot be ratified, even if the directors wish it: *Ashbury Railway Carriage Co. v. Riche* (1875). Answer **b** is incorrect because s.35 — which basically states that an *ultra vires* transaction sanctioned by the directors will bind the company — only applies if the other party acted in good faith. It's generally agreed that a banker, because he will invariably have a copy of or have had sight of a copy of a company customer's memorandum of association, could not claim to be unaware of the company's objects and borrowing powers and therefore would not be acting in good faith within the meaning of the section.

If the director expressly acted as agent for the company, the contract of loan was clearly intended to be with the company and nobody else. So, the directors are not liable on it (answer **c**). However, the director who negotiated the loan is liable for breach of warranty of authority, as is any other director who authorized the negotiation of the loan.

Subrogation — the correct answer — entitles the banker to the rights of any creditor who has been paid off using the *ultra vires* borrowing. In other words, the banker can sue the company for the amount of the loan used to pay off one or more of its legitimate creditors. He is not entitled, however, to any securities held by the creditors.

10 The correct answer is **c**.

Answers **a** and **b** both concern the extent of an agent's authority to operate an account. No authority to negotiate new overdraft facilities can be *implied* by having authority to draw cheques (answer **a**). On a joint account all parties to the account must authorize the agent to draw cheques (answer **b**).

Answer **d** (drawing cheques payable to himself) would be a classic case of negligence on the banker's part, unless he had checked that the agent was entitled to the money. Collecting such cheques would in effect mean automatic loss of protection under the Cheques Act 1957, s.4.

When an agent indorses cheques payable to his principal to another person (answer **c**) he is doing nothing unusual. Indorsing cheques is a perfectly standard procedure under the Bills of Exchange Act 1882. Therefore the banker would be acting in the normal course of business unless he had good reason to suspect that there were circumstances about the indorsement requiring investigation prior to collecting the cheques.

Score 2 marks for each correct answer. What was your score for this topic? Fill it in on the score grid.

If you scored 12 or less and are still a bit shaky on some points go back and look at the study guide again, before proceeding any further.

If you are sure you really understand and are familiar with the topic now, try the 10 further questions which are on pages 172-175.

Alternatively you can go on to the next topic and do all the post-tests together at the end.

Topic 3   Partnership

Study guide

Putting it in context

Partnerships are one of the two most important types of business organizations with which you will deal in day-to-day banking. The other is, of course, the registered company. So, this is part of the context of partnership and banking law. (We compare partnerships and registered companies in the next Topic Section.) The other thing to bear in mind is that partnership law, at least in so far as it relates to banking, is very much an application of the general rules of agency. This is reflected in the types of exam questions set; agency and partnership are often combined in one question.

How to approach it

Remember that you're revising law *relating* to banking and therefore the more general aspects of partnership law, interesting though they may be, are of secondary importance. For example, while you should be aware of how to determine whether or not two or more people are legally a partnership, a banker isn't very likely to be troubled by this question in practice. Hence there are more important things to revise.

We suggest that you structure your revision around the following main areas:

— How a partnership is *formed* and the different *types* of partners.
— The *authority* and *liability* of partners.
— The *relationship* between partners.
— *Dissolution* of partnership and its *consequences*.
— *Partnership and banking* — an application of the rest and obviously the most important.

Let's look at these one at a time.

Formation of partnership

Quite simply, a partnership is formed by agreement — a contract,

48

express or implied. Nothing difficult here. You must be able to explain what is meant by the *firm name* and outline the information about the partnership's membership which must be disclosed under the Business Names Act 1985.

Although in practical, economic and virtually all other terms, *limited partnerships* are of little importance, they seem to have a fascination for examiners, perhaps because it's easy to set questions on them! So you should know the difference between a general and a limited partner. You could draw a table to do this. Remember to include rights as well as liabilities.

The authority and liabilities of partners

Authority Can you explain and distinguish between a partner's *express* and *implied* authority? You must be able to do so. It's probably worth learning a short explanation/distinction. The case of *Mercantile Credit Co. Ltd v. Garrod* (1962) is an extremely good example of implied authority. Be able to explain briefly what happened and why the court decided as it did.

Partners in any kind of firm have some *implied authority* — in the usual course of the firm's business remember; but that of members of a trading partnership is more extensive. You should have a clear list showing this. If you haven't, make one.

Liability Liability for debts and other obligations of the firm is *joint*: PA 1890, s.9. Liability for torts authorized by the firm or committed in the ordinary course of the firm's business is *joint and several*: PA 1890, s.2.

Basically, *joint liability* gave a creditor of a firm one right of action only and this could be exercised by suing one partner, a combination of partners, or the firm jointly. Once judgment was obtained, however, he had no further right of action against any of the remaining partners, whether or not the judgment debt was satisfied.

However, since the Civil Liability (Contribution) Act 1978, the practical distinction is much less since it allows a creditor who obtains judgment against one or some parties to bring subsequent actions against others if the original judgment debt remains unsatisfied.

You may be asked something about the liability of a *retiring partner*. You should be familiar with: *novation*, the liability of the new firm being substituted for that of the old; *holding out*, where a partner knowingly lets himself appear to be still a partner; and the principle of *Scarf v. Jardine* (1882), which states that a creditor cannot take advantage of a 'holding out' situation by taking action against the firm as it is actually constituted and as he thought it was constituted, i.e. he can sue X and Y or Y and Z but not X, Y and Z.

Relationship between partners

The previous section concerned partners and outsiders; this section concerns their internal relationship. If there is no formal deed or articles of partnership, ss.19–31 of the 1890 Act provide the framework for this.

Dissolution of partnership

There are three ways in which a partnership may be dissolved: (1) *by agreement* among the partners; (2) *under the Partnership Act 1890*; and (3) *by court order*, e.g. where the court thinks that it is just and equitable to dissolve the firm.

More important to you are the *effects* of dissolution, primarily that the authority of the partners to bind the firm ceases. This has obvious implications for the partnership account but remember that one exception to this is a partner's continuing authority to act in order to wind up the business. You should be able to cite *Re Bourne* (1906) on this point.

You may possibly be asked to explain how *partnership accounts* are settled on dissolution. Well, we covered this in answer 7 of the Short Answer Test. Remember that where there are losses on capital, these must be met according to the partnership agreement and taken into account in the final settlement. Your accounting knowledge should come in useful here.

Try the following example. A, B and C contributed capital of £10,000, £6,000 and £2,000 respectively, but shared profits and losses equally. Creditors are owed £15,000 and there are undrawn profits of £6,000. Calculate the final settlement. (Answer at the foot of the page.)

The undrawn profits (£6,000) are appropriated to pay creditors leaving a balance of £9,000 (15,000 − 6,000) to be met out of capital. This means that there has been a loss of capital of £9,000. This is shared equally by the partners, hence:

	A	B	C	Total
Capital	10,000	6,000	2,000	18,000
Loss of capital	3,000	3,000	3,000	9,000
Balance	7,000	3,000	(−1,000)	9,000

A is left with £7,000 of his £10,000 and B with £3,000 of his original £6,000. C, however, must contribute £1,000 to the dissolution.

Partnership and banking

This is what is important to you, both as far as the exam and your work is concerned. This is where the general law is applied to a part of the 'real world' — in this case the business of banking. A word of warning in this topic and others. Law and banking practice invariably overlap and while it is always relevant to explain briefly how a banker would deal with something in practice, the exam primarily tests your knowledge and understanding of law. Hence the bulk of your answers should be statements, explanations and applications of legal rules.

You must be able to apply the law to the following areas.

Opening the account Why, for example, is it important for a banker to check on the *membership* of the firm? (Answer at the foot of the page.) Remember that a bank will want a mandate signed which sets out the partners authority as agents of the firm, e.g. as to borrowing powers, and that anything outside the mandate will require authorization. The bank will not just rely on the rules of agency for protection.

Joint and several liability We've already explained the difference between these and how this is less important than it once was. Remember that joint and several liability is accepted in the mandate form. But you must also be able to illustrate why. Remember the answer to question 6 in the Short Answer Test? Make a brief note of the reasons below.

Operating the account Countermanding partnership cheques, cheques which require investigation, e.g. partnerships cheques indorsed to a partner etc.

Borrowing Express and implied power to borrow and give securities, trading and non-trading partnerships. This is a favourite exam topic. While in practice the mandate will cover the situation, you must first assume that there is no express provision and explain the general principles. In particular, you should distinguish between *trading* and *non-trading* partnerships and then apply this to the question. As part of your conclusion you could explain that usual banking practice is to cover borrowing powers and securities in a *mandate* signed by all the partners.

Retirement of a partner What procedure should be adopted? A retiring partner remains liable for the firm's debts as at the date of his retirement but, in order to preserve his liability and to establish the

---

(Answer) It's important to check on the membership of the firm in order to be able to rely on the statutory protection afforded by the Cheques Act 1957, s.4 when collecting cheques.

bank's right over any security deposited by him to secure the account, the firm's account must be broken and future entries passed through a new account.

The reason for this is *Clayton's Case* (1816), a decision of great importance to bankers and something which you're *bound* to have to apply in the exam. You should *learn* the following rule.

In a current account payments-in are appropriated to debit items in chronological order, unless the customer or the banker takes steps to appropriate particular credits against particular debits.

Let's look at an example. A, B and C were in partnership. A retired with the firm's overdraft standing at £10,000. If the account had been continued unbroken and credits of £10,000 had been paid in and payments of £10,000 made, the debit balance for which A was liable would have been completely extinguished, through the operation of the Rule, although the overdraft itself would have remained at £10,000. The difference would be that now only B and C would be liable on it. Let's look at the Rule operating on a bank statement (below). A retires on 1 January when the firm's liabilities stand at £10,000. By 20 January, £10,000 has been paid into the account and this completely extinguishes his liability, even though the account is still £5,000 overdrawn and £10,000 overdrawn the following day. By simply ruling off the account at his retirement and opening a new account, the operation of the Rule is avoided.

Payments	Receipts	Date	Balance
5,000		1/1	10,000 DR
		(A retires.)	
	1,000	10/1	9,000 DR
5,000		12/1	14,000 DR
	6,000	15/1	8,000 DR
	3,000	20/1	5,000 DR
5,000		21/1	10,000 DR

You'd be amazed how many students seem never to have heard of the Rule in *Clayton's Case*, of those that have, few seem to be able to state and explain it. You must be able to do so, so *learn* it. You'll come across the Rule again in several other Topics.

Death of a partner   What procedure should be adopted? Why is *Clayton's Case* important? (Write a brief answer to these questions — you *must* be able to do this.)

Bankruptcy   Once again, what procedure should be adopted and why?

Can you explain? This is a common question and you should be able to state the gist of the Bankruptcy Act 1914, s.33.

— Joint estate is used first to pay joint creditors.
— Separate estates are used first to pay the separate creditors of each partner.
— A surplus on any separate estate is dealt with as joint estate.
— Any surplus on the joint estate is divided among the separate estates of the partners in proportion to their capital contribution.

Remember that, under the mandate, the partners will have assumed joint and several liability to the bank giving it a claim against both the joint estate and the separate estates of each partner.

Work through the following example. A receiving order is made against a partnership consisting of X, Y and Z. The assets are £50,000 and the liabilities are £80,000. X has private assets of £30,000 and liabilities of £20,000, Y has private assets of £24,000 and liabilities of £24,000, and Z has private assets of £6,000 and liabilities of £12,000. The settlement is as follows:

Partners		X	Y	Z
Assets		30,000	24,000	6,000
Liabilities		20,000	24,000	12,000
		10,000	Nil	(−6,000)
Partnership				
Assets	£50,000 + £10,000	(A) = £60,000		
Liabilities	£80,000	= £80,000		

The settlement means that X's creditors are paid in full and a surplus of £10,000 is transferred to the firm's estate. Y's creditors are also paid in full but nothing remains to transfer to the firm's estate. Z's creditors, however, receive a dividend of only 50p in the pound. The firm's assets, increased by the contribution from X's estate, give its creditors a dividend of 75p in the pound. If you are asked to state how much the creditors actually receive, this requires only a simple additional step involving a little arithmetic. (Remember that joint and several liability to their bank would have been accepted by the partners, making the above settlement academic as far as any debts to the bank are concerned.)

Now work through the revision diagrams which follow (Figs. 3.1 and 3.2).

Once you feel confident about your knowledge of this topic, try to answer the 10 multiple choice questions which follow.

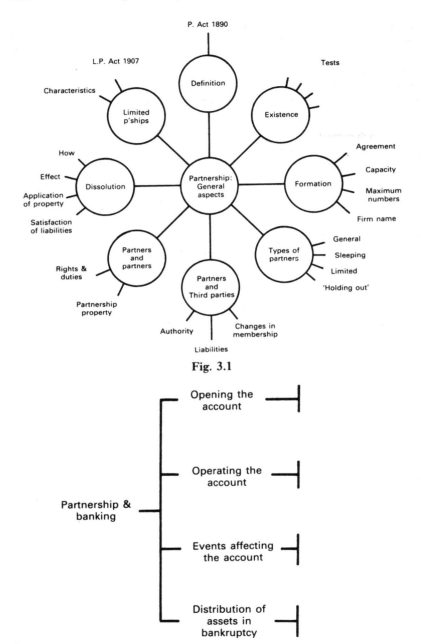

Fig. 3.1

Fig. 3.2 *Complete the above diagram*

Multiple choice questions

1 Which of the following is the best test for the existence of a partnership:

   a co-ownership of property?
   b sharing of gross returns?
   c sharing of profits?
   d sharing of profits and losses?

1 A limited partner is:

   a entitled to share in the profits of a firm but not to take part in its management.
   b entitled to share in the profits of the firm but must share any losses equally with the other partners.
   c one who contributes less than the other partners to the firm's capital.
   d one who takes no part in the firm's management but who nevertheless contributes capital and shares profits and losses in the same way as a general partner.

3 A partner's implied authority does not extend to:

   a receiving payment of debts.
   b drawing cheques.
   c borrowing money.
   d giving a guarantee in the firm name

4 A retiring partner continues to remain liable for the existing debts of the firm unless:

   a the Rule in *Clayton's Case* applies.
   b a contract of novation has been entered into.

c notice of his retirement is published in *London Gazette*.

d he gives actual notice of his retirement to existing clients.

5 If a bank accepts an assignment of a partner's share in the firm as security for a loan, it is:

a entitled to share in the profits of the firm.

b entitled to take part in the management of the firm.

c able to enter into contracts on the firm's behalf.

d liable for the firm's debts.

6 The Partnership Act 1890 specifies certain events and situations which will dissolve a partnership and others which empower the court to order a dissolution. The latter category includes:

a the death or bankruptcy of any partner.

b the charging of a partner's share in the firm by the court as security for his judgment debts.

c where the firm's business becomes unlawful.

d where any partner is guilty of conduct prejudicial to the firm's business.

7 X, Y and Z contributed capital of £5,000, £3,000 and £1,000 respectively but shared profits and losses equally. Creditors are owed £6,000 and Z made a loan to the firm which, with interest accrued, now totals £3,000. There are no undrawn profits. The final settlement on dissolution is:

a X: £2,000, Y: Nil, Z: £1,000.

b X: £2,000, Y: Nil, Z: (−£2,000).

c X: Nil, Y: Nil, Z: Nil.

d X: £3,000, Y: £1,000, Z: (−£1,000).

8 Joint and several liability is accepted by partners in the bank mandate form in order:

   a to avoid the Rule in *Kendall v. Hamilton* (1879).

   b to ensure that all partners are liable for the firm's debts.

   c that security deposited by a partner for all personal liabilities may be appropriated by the bank against either his personal debt or the partnership debt.

   d to give each partner express power to borrow on the firm's behalf.

answer

9 The case of *Devaynes v. Noble* was decided in:

   a 1761.

   b 1861.

   c 1816.

   d 1916.

answer

10 A receiving order is made against the firm of ABC & Co. The assets are £25,000 and the liabilities are £50,000. A has separate assets of £30,000 and separate debts of £15,000, B has separate assets of £25,000 and separate debts of £15,000, and C has separate assets of £20,000 and separate debts of £20,000. The firm's creditors therefore receive a dividend of:

   a 50p in the pound.

   b 75p in the pound.

   c 80p in the pound.

   d 100p in the pound.

answer

Answers follow on pages 58-61. Score 2 marks for each correct answer.

Answers

1 The correct answer is **d**.

In fact s.2 of the 1890 Act specifically states that answers **a**, **b** and **c** do not of themselves create a partnership between two or more persons and the correct answer cannot really be described as a 'test'. Each case must be decided on its own facts and the sharing of profits and losses is only a guide. However, it is a good indication of people 'trading in common' because it indicates that they are putting their trust in one another. *Keith Spicer Ltd v. Mansell* (1970) is an often quoted example of having to determine whether or not a partnership existed. It's also typical in that the question usually only has to be answered when an attempt is made to hold one person liable for the acts of another.

2 The correct answer is **a**.

Answer **d** can be quickly disposed of; this is the definition of a sleeping or dormant partner, and answer **c** could equally apply to a general partner — it's common to find partners contributing capital unequally.

Answer **b** is really the exact opposite of a limited partner; the whole idea is that he is only liable to the extent of his capital contribution. This is the characteristic of a limited partner and while answer **a** is perfectly correct it is not actually a definition. We could equally well have said that a limited partner is not an agent of the firm and that his death, bankruptcy or mental disorder do not dissolve it.

3 The correct answer is **d**.

You should have spotted that the answers distinguished between partners in non-trading and trading partnerships. A partner's implied authority is, as you'll recall, his or her authority to act, and thereby bind the firm, within the usual course of its business, irrespective of any internal limit on that authority.

Receiving payment of debts and drawing cheques (answers **a** and **b**) are both considered by the law to be part and parcel of the activities of any firm, as are buying and selling goods and engaging employees. Borrowing money (answer **d**) is only considered part and parcel of a trading partnership's activities and hence a member of a non-trading firm must be expressly authorized to do this. However, authority to give a guarantee in the firm name will never be implied in any kind of partnership. Thus, if a firm wishes to give a guarantee to a bank, the guarantee must be signed by all the members of the firm.

4 The correct answer is **b**.

Did you read the question carefully? It specifically referred to existing debts. Publishing notice of his retirement in the *London Gazette* (answer **c**) or giving actual notice to existing clients (answer **d**) makes absolutely no difference to the liabilities which already exist. Giving notice in these ways ensures that he does not incur liability for future debts.

The Rule in *Clayton's Case* (1816) (answer **a**) is relevant to the situation since a retiring partner's liabilities would be extinguished by the Rule merely through payments into the current account in the ordinary course of business. However, banks invariably break the account on receiving notice of a retirement and thereby preserve liability for existing debts. You must know and be able to explain the Rule.

Novation, the correct answer, is a tri-partite agreement between the retiring partner, the new firm, i.e. the old firm minus the retiring partner and/or plus any new partner(s), and the existing creditors under which the creditors release the retiring partner from his liabilities in consideration of the new firm accepting them.

5 The correct answer is **a**.

Assignment is the legal process by which certain rights are transferred from one peson to another. For example, a legal mortgage of a life policy is effected by an assignment of the policy.

Although perhaps uncommon, a partner's share in the firm can be assigned as a security. Now, if this is done, the assignee (the bank) is really only interested in the value of that share and the profits the firm may make. So, it is basic to the arrangement that he becomes entitled to the assignor's share of the profits (answer **a**). (A partner's share, by the way, is that proportion of the proceeds of the notional sale of the firm's assets to which he would be entitled after the firm's debts have been paid.

The assignee doesn't become a member of the firm so he can neither take part in its management (answer **b**) nor act as its agent (answer **c**). A bank would ensure that the assignment did not make it liable for the firm's debts (answer **d**).

6 The correct answer is **d**.

A partnership can be dissolved in three ways: by agreement; under the 1890 Act; by the Court. Answers **a**, **b** and **c** are all situations specified in the Act, although it's worth remembering that while in **a** and **b** the dissolution is automatic under the act, it's also at the option of the other partners and may well have been covered by the firm's formal articles or deed of partnership.

The court's powers relate to situations for which it would be difficult to legislate. How do you lay down in an Act criteria to determine whether it's 'just and equitable' to dissolve a firm — another situation in which the court has jurisdiction? Similarly, it's a question of fact whether particular conduct is prejudicial to the firm's business (answer **d**). (You'll find some amusing examples if you ever have the chance to read a book on partnership law!)

7 The correct answer is **b**.

Work through the following solution. Creditors must be paid first. This means a loss of capital of £6,000. Next, Z's loan, with interest accrued on it, must be repaid, adding a further loss of capital of £3,000 making £9,000 in total. This loss must be shared equally by the partners and gives the following settlement.

	X	Y	Z	Total
Capital	£5,000	£3,000	£1,000	£9,000
Loss of capital	£3,000	£3,000	£3,000	£9,000
Balance	£2,000	Nil	(£–2,000)	Nil

Hence, X is left with £2,000, Y with nothing and Z must contribute £2,000, although, of course, he has already received the repayment of his loan to the firm.

8 The correct answer is **c**.

This is one of the four reasons you should have noted down in the Study Guide to this Topic. If you didn't, be sure to do so when you've finished going through the remaining answers.

We can dispose of the other options quite simply. The Rule in *Kendall v. Hamilton* (1879) (answer **a**), which prevented subsequent actions once judgment was obtained against one or more persons jointly liable on a debt, was overruled by the Civil Liability (Contribution) Act 1978. Hence, joint and several liability is no longer imposed for this reason. Answer **b** is just incorrect; imposing joint and several liability doesn't of itself ensure that all partners are liable for the firm's debts. This is done by checking on its membership and ensuring that all members sign the mandate. Again, power to borrow (answer **d**) is something covered by the mandate. The nature of the liability assumed by the partners has no bearing on their authority in any particular matter.

9   The correct answer is **c**

Normally, you won't lose marks if you can't remember the dates of the cases that you cite in your answers. However, there are a few cases where the examiner may expect you to know the year in which they were decided. *Clayton's Case* (1816), is one. (As a rule of thumb, try to remember the dates of cases which established an important principle and those of recent decisions.) Remember, it's absolutely vital that you know this Rule and can explain and apply it without having to think about it.

10   The correct answer is **d.**

Work through the following settlement.

Partners	A	B	C
Assets	£30,000	£25,000	£20,000
Liabilities	£15,000	£15,000	£20,000
	£15,000	£10,000	£Nil

Partnership		
Assets	£25,000 + £15,000 + £10,000 = £50,000
Liabilities	= £50,000

You can see from this settlement that assets are equal to liabilities and therefore creditors are paid in full, 100p in the pound.

Score 2 marks for each corret answer. What was your score for this topic? Fill it in on the score grid.

If you scored 12 or less and are still a bit shaky on some points go back and look at the study guide again, before proceeding any further.

If you are sure you really understand and are familiar with the topic now, try the 10 further questions which are on pages 175-177.

Alternatively you can go on to the next topic and do all the post-tests together at the end.

Topic 4   Companies

Study guide

Companies and banking law is one of the largest and more complicated topics in the syllabus, so it's as well to have plenty of time and be 'on the ball' when tackling it.

Perhaps the first thing to do when confronted with a large topic to revise is to divide it up into more manageable sections and consider each in terms of relative importance. You can divide your revision of companies, for example, into the following sections:

1   The nature of a company, its formation and operation.
2   The capital of a company.
3   Company bank accounts.
4   Company borrowing.
5   Securities.
6   Debentures.
7   Winding-up.

Quite a list but at least you can now begin to see the framework of the topic. Of these sections, it's 3–7 on which you are most likely to be set questions, and sections 4 and 5 in particular.

Companies: some basic points

Companies Act 1985   It's worth mentioning right at the start that all company legislation was *consolidated* in the Companies Act 1985. The law hasn't been re-written but section numbers have changed. Make sure that your references are to the 1985 Act and not earlier ones.

Companies and partnerships   It's conventional to begin company law with a company's separate legal personality (*Salomon v. Salomon & Co* (1897)) and make comparisons with a partnership. Occasionally you're asked a question involving this. If you haven't already got one, make a table comparing a registered company with a partnership.

Classifications   Virtually all trading companies were registered under one of the Companies Acts and they can be classified according to the *limit*, if any, on the *shareholders' liability* to contribute towards payment of the company's debts, or according to whether the company is a *public* company or a *private* company: something that you must understand but points on which you're unlikely to be questioned.

Memorandum and articles of association You certainly need to know about a company's memorandum and articles of association — the documents in which the constitution and rules of the company are found. The objects clause and the *ultra vires* rule must be understood and you should be able to cite and explain *Ashbury Railway Carriage and Iron Co v. Riche* (1895), or a later case, and *Introductions Ltd v. National Provincial Bank Ltd* (1970), surely an unforgettable case!

Although a bank would never be able to rely on it in practice, the modification of the *ultra vires* rule by the s.35 (originally s.9(1) of the European Communities Act 1972) is important, e.g. in relation to company borrowing. It's well worth making a summary of the effects of s.35 and learning it. *Turquand's Case* (1856) in relation to the articles and, indeed, s.35 is also worth summarizing and learning.

The operation of a company A company acts through its directors; they are its executive controllers and agents although, as was shown in *Panorama Developments v. Fidelis Furnishing Fabrics Ltd* (1971), its secretary may have implied authority to act as its agent in certain circumstances.

The aspect of a company's operation with which a banker is most concerned is the conduct of board meetings, quorums in particular. A *quorum* in this context is the number of directors which must be present at a board meeting to make the proceedings valid. This is especially relevant when a banker *lends money* or *takes security* from a company. Be sure you know and can explain the following in this context:

— The standard banking practice of submitting *draft resolutions* for the board's approval.
— The role of *Turquand's Case* (1856).
— The problem of *interested directors*.

Make notes if necessary.

Loans and guarantees Power to make loans and give guarantees is determined by a company's memorandum of association but strict *statutory restrictions* are imposed on loans made by companies, e.g. to directors or to assist a person to purchase its own shares. Do you know them?

The capital of a company

Shares and debentures Note the main *distinctions* between shares and debentures — you should be able to think of at least two.

Alteration A company can alter its share capital. An increase or alteration doesn't really affect a bank but a reduction in share capital would do where a loan has been granted on the security of its shares. This is because the value of the securities would be automatically reduced. However, a reduction in share capital needs the court's sanction and any creditors affected can object.

Company bank accounts

Perhaps more practice of banking than banking law, but you should know:

— The procedure for *opening* an account, particularly the contents of the mandate.
— The rules for *operating* the account, particularly 'per pro' signatures, and possible types of misuse of the account by directors.

Company borrowing

A topic that you must know thoroughly. You should start with the *objects clause*: are there express borrowing powers? If so, what are they? Remember that a *trading company* has implied power both to borrow and to give security for its debts. Next, what limits, if any, are imposed on the borrowing powers of *directors* in the articles.

Ultra vires borrowing As far as the exam is concerned, this is possibly the most important topic here. Learn the following basic principle.

Any advance which is ultra vires the company is *void*, as is any security given to cover the advance. Ratification of it is not possible.

It would be an excellent idea to 'prepare' this topic on a separate piece of paper and make it part of your revision notes. You should then know the following. Make *brief* notes on each.

— The effect of *s.35*.
— A banker's *remedies* (four of them) where a loan proves to be ultra vires.
— Borrowing in which the *directors* act outside the company's articles:
Additional remedies
When can a banker rely on the Rule in *Turquand's Case* (1856).

Securities

Another topic that you must know thoroughly, and once again it would be a good idea to 'prepare' it for the exam.

Registrable charges are defined in s.395, which also imposes the 21 day period in which registration must be effected. Make notes on the following points.

— *Registrable charges* Pay particular attention to charges over land — registered and unregistered. (While it's perhaps easier to remember which charges don't need to be registered and then assume that all others do, you really need a list of the main ones which are registrable.)

— *Registration* The basic 21 day period under s.395 and extension and rectification of it under s.404; the effect of s.401, and the consequences of non-registration or registration out of time.

Debentures

Debentures are documents issued by a company acknowledging a loan and any charge securing it. (It's always worth learning definitions off by heart.)

Bank debenture forms We've already asked you a question on the type of debentures taken by banks. Just in case you don't remember, a banker will invariably take an *all-moneys* debenture on his standard terms. This is because such a debenture will secure all moneys owing on any account at any time, and will always keep pace with the overdrawn balance.

What are the *usual provisions* in a banker's debenture form? You're unlikely to be asked to list them but, if presented with one or more, you must be able to explain why they are included.

Fixed and floating charges Learn definitions of these and the distinctions between them. What is meant by *crystallization* of a floating charge and when does it occur?

The *defects of a floating charge* make a good question. We're listing the main ones below — be sure you can explain them in some detail.

— *Running down of assets.*
— *Fixed charges* have priority.
— *Romalpa clauses* — you must know the basic principles behind

them but it would be unfair to ask you about the finer points of case law on them.

— *Invalidation by the Insolvency Act 1985, s. 104, Clayton's Case* (1816) is relevant here; it actually assists a bank — how? *Re Yeovil Glove Co Ltd* (1965) is a good example.

— *Invalidation by the Insolvency Act 1985, s.101* — voidable preferences.

Remedies of a debenture holder What are they and when can they be exercised?

Winding-up

There are two ways in which a company can be wound-up: compulsorily by the court and voluntarily.

Compulsory winding-up A company is usually subject to a compulsory winding-up order under s.517 because it can't pay its debts, a creditor owed at least £750 having made a proper demand for payment and having remained unpaid for three weeks.

Under s.524, compulsory winding-up *commences* either at the time the petition is presented to the court, or when a resolution to wind-up voluntarily was passed if the company was in voluntary liquidation before the petition was presented.

From a banker's point of view, the most important *consequences* of a compulsory winding-up are:

— Any *disposition of property* made after its commencement is void unless sanctioned by the court: s.522. This includes transfers of shares, credits to the account and the payment of third party cheques. You should be able to cite *Re Grays Inn Construction Co Ltd* (1980) here.

— *Floating charges* granted within the previous 12 months prior to the commencement of the winding-up may be void.

— The *Official Receiver* becomes the provisional liquidator.

— The *banker–customer relationship* is ended.

If you're asked a question on this, it's likely to involve the problem period, caused by the operation of s.522 (above), between the petition being presented and the winding-up order being made. Cheques to 'cash' or to 'wages' can be paid but what of third party cheques? Consider *Re Operator Control Cabs Ltd* (1970) and the *Grays Inn Case* (1980). Fortunately, this problem doesn't arise in voluntary liquidations. Herre liquidation commences when the resolution to do so is passed. The vast majority of liquidations are of this type.

Voluntary winding-up This is effectively controlled by the shareholders when the company is solvent and by the creditors when it isn't. Remember that the winding-up commences as soon as the resolution is passed. The liquidator is usually appointed immediately and takes control of the company's accounts.

Voluntary arrangements These can be made under either the Companies Act 1985 or the Insolvency Act 1985. Such arrangements do not, as such, involve the liquidation of the company, although this may ultimately follow.

Administration orders These are made under the Insolvency Act 1985, s.28 and provide an alternative to liquidation where a company is in serious financial difficulties and a receiver cannot be appointed because no floating charges exist. The court's protection of the assets is gained while an attempt is made to sort out the company and its creditors.

Associated concepts Can you define and explain the following:

— Transactions at an undervalue and Preferences: Insolvency Act 1985, s.101.
— Fraudulent trading (Companies Act 1985, s.630) and wrongful trading (Insolvency Act 1985, s.15).
— Transactions defrauding creditors: Insolvency Act 1985, s.212.
— Extortionate credit transactions: Insolvency Act 1985, s.103.

Creditors Very probably, one or more banks will be a creditor when a company goes into liquidation. Be sure that you know:

— *Rights of set-off: National Westminster Bank Ltd v. Halesowen Presswork and Assemblies* (1972).
— The options open to a *secured creditor*, e.g. a bank.
— Who are *preferential creditors?* Remember that by s.89 of the Insolvency Act 1985, any creditor, e.g. a bank, who advances money to pay wages, salaries or accrued holiday pay to the company's employees is a preferential creditor to the extent to which the advance is actually used to satisfy these preferential claims. This is a main reason why wages accounts are opened.
— The *order of distribution* of assets.

Now work through the revision diagram in Fig. 4.1. We've chosen to select just a part of the topic to summarize in the diagram. The topic is large and remember that we said that diagrams quickly lose their effect if you try to put too much on them. A useful exercise for you would be to construct diagrams covering general aspects of company law and operation and the winding-up of companies.

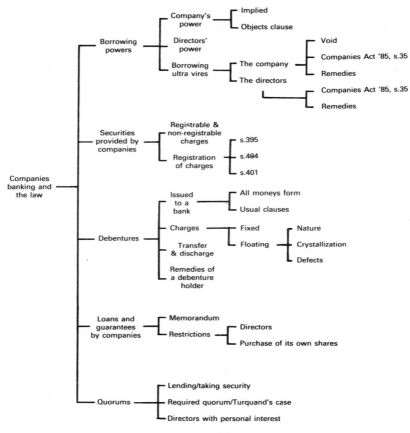

Fig. 4.1

Once you feel confident about your knowledge of this topic, try to answer the 10 multiple choice questions which follow.

Multiple choice questions

1 A public company is distinguished from a private company in that a:

    a public company must have at least seven members.

    b private company's articles of association will restrict the right of members to transfer their shares.

    c private company need not have a share capital.

    d public company has a minimum authorized and allotted share capital of (at present) £50,000.

 _answer_

2 The *ultra vires* rule primarily relates to a company's:

    a memorandum of association.

    b articles of association.

    c business certificate.

    d bank mandate form.

 _answer_

3 A company may make a loan or give a guarantee to one of its directors:

    a if its memorandum of association contains such a power.

    b provided the prior approval of the Registrar of Companies is obtained.

    c provided it is sanctioned by a quorum of the other directors.

    d if the director is its holding company.

 _answer_

4 If a banker lends money to a company for an *ultra vires* purpose, he can:

    a do nothing to recover the money.

    b be subrogated to the rights of certain creditors.

c   rely on the Companies Act 1985, s.35.

d   rely on the Rule in *Turquand's Case* (1856).

5   Registrable charges are governed by the Companies Act 1985:

a   s.95.

b   s.117.

c   s.395.

d   s.404.

6   The period prescribed by the Companies Act 1985 for the registration of charges is:

a   7 days.

b   14 days.

c   21 days.

d   28 days.

7   Which of following securities does not require registration with the Registrar of Companies:

a   a charge on land?

b   a charge on a life policy?

c   a floating charge?

d   a charge on uncalled share capital.

8   A banker's debenture form giving the bank a floating charge on the company's assets will include an 'all money's clause' in order to avoid:

a   possible difficulties with a 'Romalpa clause'.

b   section 104 of the Insolvency Act 1985.

c   fixed charges taking priority.

d   problems caused by a fluctuating overdraft.

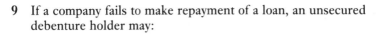

9   If a company fails to make repayment of a loan, an unsecured
    debenture holder may:

    a   appoint a receiver.
    b   petition for a winding-up order.
    c   sell the company's assets.
    d   take possession of the assets and continue the business.

10 XYZ & Co is insolvent and in its liquidation there are the following
    claimants:
        i   Bank A holding a legal mortgage on its premises.
        ii   Bank B holding a floating charge over its stock and other
             assets.
        iii The local authority for unpaid rates for a period of six
             months.
        iv   The liquidator for his expenses.
    The order of distribution of XYZ & Co's assets is:

    a   i, ii, iii, iv.
    b   ii, iv, iii, i.
    c   i, iv, iii, ii.
    d   i, iv, ii, iii.

Answers follow on pages 72-77. Score 2 marks for each correct
answer.

Answers

1   The correcct answer is **c**.

The first point to make is that the main distinctions between public and private companies were not options given to you. In fact these are that:

— only a public company can offer its shares and debentures to the general public,
— a public company must have at least two directors, a private company can have only one,
— a public company requires a 'business certificate' before it can start operating.

So, let's look at the options given to you. If you chose answer **a** (the number of members) you must be using a very old textbook! For quite a few years now, two is the minimum membership for any kind of company. Similarly, restrictions on the transfer of shares (answer **b**), while still commonly found in the articles of private companies, is not part of the legal distinction.

Public companies do indeed have to have a minimum authorized and allotted share capital of (at present) £50,000 (answer **d**), so if you chose this answer it's understandable. However, many private companies have share capitals well above this figure so it's not asbolutely correct.

This leaves **c**, the fact that a private company need not have a share capital. Such a company would be one limited by guarantee.

2   The correct answer is **a**.

Ultra vires means 'beyond the powers of'. When applied to a company it relates primarily to the objects clause of its memorandum of association. This clause sets out what the company can do. So **a** is the correct answer. Any act of the company which is *ultra vires*, e.g. a contract or a loan for an *ultra vires* purpose, is void and cannot be enforced against the company.

A word about the other options: the articles of association, together with the memorandum of association, comprise a company's constitution, the memorandum dealing with its external affairs, and the articles with its internal affairs. The business certificate is issued by the Registrar of Companies under the Companies Act 1985. A public company cannot commence business or operate a bank account without one. Bank mandate forms must be signed by the chairman and secretary of the company and cover all banking operations relating to the account and specify who has authority to operate it. Clearly the account must only be operated in strict accordance with it.

3 The correct answer is **d**.

The making of loans to directors and guaranteeing loans made by others to them are activities which are strictly regulated by statute. A moment's reflection should tell you that if the position was otherwise the opportunites for fraud and general malpractice would be endless. This being the case, answers **a** and **c** would both give far too wide a scope to a company bent on such malpractices.

This leaves answers **b** and **d**. The Registrar of Companies has an immensely important role in the law and operation of companies, e.g. maintaining registers of charges created by companies, but sanctioning loans and guarantees is not one of his functions. It would almost certainly be an impossible task for him and his staff in any case.

The Companies Act 1985, ss.330(2) contains a general prohibition on companies making loans to their directors and giving guarantees or other securities for loans to their directors from other persons, but with a number of exceptions (ss.322–8). A loan by a subsidiary company to its holding company, the latter being a director of the former, or a loan not exceeding £2,500 being two exceptions. Another is where lending money and giving guarantees is part of the company's ordinary course of business and the loan or guarantee is made in the ordinary course of that business. Hence, a bank can grant overdrafts to its directors!

4 The correct answer is **b**.

In the answer to question 2 we explained the meaning and effect of the *ultra vires* rule. As far as a banker is concerned, it's of most direct relevance where company borrowing is concerned. Remember *Introductions Ltd v. National Provincial Bank Ltd* (1970), where the bank lent money to the company to develop its pig-breeding enterprise when its objects clause was all about providing facilities for foreign visitors? Its worth reading a report of the case, since it illustrates that borrowing money is *not* an independent activity, whatever the memorandum might say — it relates to its other stated objects. Another point to remember, and something to watch for in the exam, is that borrowing may be merely *ultra vires* the directors and not the company itself; a bank's position differs accordingly. If you're not sure of this, it's something to revise thoroughly.

So now to the question itself. Answer **a** is just wrong: a banker has remedies open to him which may enable him to recover the money lent. (Remember, however, that the loan itself and any security given for it is void and cannot be the basis for legal action.) One such remedy is answer **b**, the correct answer. If the company uses any of the money to pay off its creditors, a banker is subrogated to the rights of (stands in the shoes of) those creditors who have been paid off. In other words, the bank replaces them as the company's creditors.

The Companies Act 1985, s.35, answer **c**, provides in favour of a person dealing with the company in good faith that 'the power of the directors to bind the company shall be deemed to be free of any limitation under the memorandum or articles of association.' It further provides that no enquiry need be made into possible limits on the directors' powers and that a third party is presumed to have acted in good faith unless the contrary can be proved. However, in *International Sales Agencies Ltd and Another v. Marcus and Another* (1982) it was held that a person would not be acting in good faith where in all the circumstances of the case he could not reasonably have been unaware of the *ultra vires* nature of the transaction. Now, since a bank will receive or at least inspect a copy of the memorandum and articles before opening the account, it is improbable that a bank could ever rely on s.35.

The Rule in *Turquand's Case* (1856) (answer **d**) states that a person dealing with a company is taken to know the contents of its memorandum and articles of association and he must ensure that the proposed transaction is consistent with them. He may, however, assume that the company has properly completed any internal formalities which may be required before the transaction can be entered into by the company. This rule would apply, for example, to a transaction which is not sanctioned by the directors, or which is sanctioned by an improperly conducted board meeting. However, it doesn't, indeed cannot, render enforceable a loan or any other transaction which is *ultra vires* and therefore void.

5   The correct answer is **c**.

This explanation is as short as the previous one was long! A straightforward question: one right answer and three wrong.

If you chose answer **a** (s.95) you've probably got out-of-date notes. This was the relevant section in the Companies Act 1948, now consolidated with other company legislation in the Companies Act 1985. Section 117 (answer **b**) in the section which requires a 'business certificate' to be issued to a public company by the Registrar of Companies before it can commence trading. Section 404 (answer **d**) does deal with the registration of charges but empowers the court to extend the 21 day period prescribed by s.395 when it is satisfied that failure to register was accidental or due to inadvertence or some other sufficient cause; or will not prejudice the creditors or shareholders; or on other grounds where it is just and equitable to grant relief.

6 The correct answer is **c**.

Another straightforward question: 21 days is the registration period under S.395. We did in fact mention this in the previous answer and also discussed s.404. Taking securities from companies is a common exam question, not least of all because there is a straightforward basic principle and just the set of exceptions to it on which to base questions. So, be sure you know:

— Section 395: registration of a charge must be within 21 days of its creation. See *Esberger & Son Ltd v. Capital & Counties Bank* (1913).

— Section 404: extension of the 21 day period by the court. See *Re Kris Cruisers Ltd* (1949).

— Section 401: the Registrar's certificate of registration of the charge is conclusive evidence of compliance with the statutory requirements.

7 The correct answer is **b**.

As we said in the Study Guide, most charges created by companies are registrable. Even the most informal charge on land (answer **a**) must be registered, e.g. a letter undertaking to deposit title deeds as security. Remember also that a charge by a company over registered land must be entered on the Charges Register at the Land Registry and a charge by a company over unregistered land unsupported by a deposit of title deeds must be entered on the Land Charges Register unless it is a floating charge. Non-registration of a charge over land, or any other registrable security, doesn't invalidate the loan, merely the charge securing it, the lender becoming an unsecured creditor.

Besides a charge on a life policy, the other non-registrable charges are those on produce, stocks and shares, negotiable instruments and ECGD policies.

8 The correct answer is **d**

When a company is granted loan facilities it is highly improbable that its financial requirements will remain constant; the overdrawn balance will fluctuate in the ordinary course of business. Quite simply, an 'all moneys' clause in a debenture ensures that the security covers all amounts owing on any account at any time, automatically keeping pace with fluctuations in cash flow etc.

All three of the other answers deal with very real problems associated with a floating charge — a likely exam question — but the 'all moneys' clause cannot be a protection against them. In a contract for the supply of goods, a Romalpa clause (answer **a**) will mean that the seller retains title to the goods in certain circumstances until he has been fully paid. Quite a reasonable precaution but it prejudices a banker's position if he has a floating charge on the buyer's assets. The goods covered by the clause don't form part of them and he has no way of knowing this unless his customer tells him.

 You'll find a concise summary of the current position with such clauses in *The Law of Banking*, chapter 4: Palfreman: Pitman)

Answer **b** (Insolvency Act 1985, s.104) 'prevents' insolvent companies from creating floating charges to secure past debts to the prejudice of their other unsecured creditors. It provides that unless consideration is received by the company at the same time as or after the charge is created, it is invalidated on the application of the liquidator or administrator if it was created within the following periods before the commencement of a liquidation or the application for an administration order: two years — in favour of a connected person; one year — in favour of any other person, provided in this latter case, at the time the charge was created the company was unable to pay its debts or became unable to pay its debts as a result of the transaction under which the charge was created.

Fixed charges (answer **c**) take priority over floating charges provided the fixed charge was taken for value and without notice of any prohibition or restriction in the original debenture on the company's power to create such a charge. A bank holding a floating charge can protect its position by including the restriction on Form 395 when registering the debenture with the Registrar of Companies.

9 The correct answer is **b**.

The first point to make is that a banker would never take an unsecured debenture willingly, so this is definitely theory rather than practice. Now, an unsecured debenture holder has no rights against any of the company's property — the very essence of taking security — and so options **a**, **c** and **d** are not open to him. As a secured debenture holder, however, these rights will be expressly included in a bank's debenture.

Since a debenture itself is no more than a document acknowledging a loan and any charge securing it, an unsecured debenture holder is merely an unsecured creditor who happens to hold excellent documentary evidence of the debt owed to him. This being so, the two remedies open to him are to (i) sue for the principal and interest due, and (ii) petition for the winding-up of the company on the ground that it is unable to pay its debts.

10   The correct answer is **d**.

In the liquidation of an insolvent company, the order of distribution of assets is:

— To creditors secured by fixed charges, from the securities charged to them.
— To the costs of the liquidation.
— To the preferential creditors.
— To debenture holders secured by floating charges.
— To unsecured creditors.

Applying this to the question, Bank A (**i**) is secured by a fixed charge and so has priority followed by the liquidator (**iv**). The local authority's claim (**iii**) for unpaid rates is no longer a preferential claim under the Insolvency Act 1985 and therefore Bank B's floating charge (**ii**) takes priority over it. This gives the final order of priority: i, iv, ii, iii.

The distribution of assets on winding-up makes a good exam question, both sorting out the order and working out who gets paid how much. It's well worth learning thoroughly, particularly the types of preferential creditors. Don't forget that s.89 of the Insolvency Act 1985 gives preferential status to a creditor who advances money to pay wages, salaries or accrued holiday pay to the company's employees to the extent to which his advance is actually used to satisfy these preferential claims.

Score 2 marks for each correct answer. What was your score for this topic? Fill it in on the score grid.

If you scored 12 or less and are still a bit shaky on some points go back and look at the study guide again, before proceeding any further.

If you are sure you really understand and are familiar with the topic now, try the 10 further questions which are on pages 177-180.

Alternatively you can go on to the next topic and do all the post-tests together at the end.

Topic 5   Bankruptcy

Study guide

Companies go into liquidation (winding-up), sole traders, other individuals and partnerships are made bankrupt. But there are common features. In both processes insolvency is involved (!) and certain aspects are common, e.g. fraudulent preferences. However, the whole structure of bankruptcy law will change when the relevant sections of the Insolvency Act 1985 come into force.

What is bankruptcy?

As always, a basic definition is a good place to start.

> Bankruptcy is the legal process by which the estate (property) of an insolvent person is taken in to the control of a trustee who uses it to pay off the debts owed to creditors of that person.

The law is at present contained in the Bankruptcy Act 1914, as amended by the Bankruptcy (Amendment) Act 1926 and the Insolvency Act 1976.

Bankruptcy starts with the debtor committing one of ten *acts of bankruptcy*.

 Can you list them? Have a go! Complete the list and check it with your notes or text book *before* reading on.

You should pay particular attention to the following; they are particularly suitable for questions:

— Fraudulent conveyances.
— Fraudulend preferences.

The bankruptcy process

This can be summarized by a 'flowchart' (Fig. 5.1). Take each item in turn in the chart, think about it, go back to your notes or textbook if necessary, go on to the next and repeat the process. Annotate (add notes or prompts etc.) to the chart if you wish.

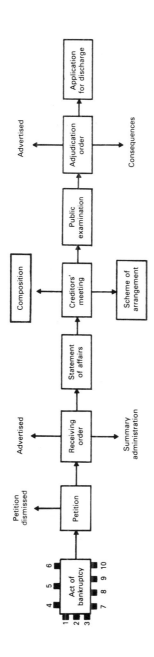

Fig. 5.1 *The bankruptcy proces*

The debtor's property

The *adjudication order* vests title to a bankrupt's property in his trustee in bankruptcy. This is the basic principle. However, the availability of property for distribution is complicated by a number of important rules.

1. *The doctrine of relation back* Bankruptcy commences on the date of the first available act of bankruptcy committed in the *three months* immediately preceding the presentation of the bankruptcy petition: Bankruptcy Act 1914, s.37. This means that any property that belonged to the debtor that has been transferred since the first available act, but which if retained would have been divisible among creditors, can be recovered by the trustee from its present owner! If you're not sure how this principle works, Fig. 5.2 should show you.

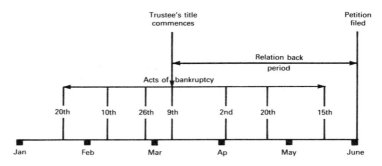

Fig. 5.2 *Relation back*

2. *Recoverable property* This principle can extend the trustee's title back beyond the three months provided by the doctrine of relation back. It applies to:

— fraudulent conveyances,
— voluntary settlements,
— fraudulent preferences,
— general assignments of book debts.

3. *Non-divisible property* This is property which the debtor can keep, e.g. personal earnings necessary to support him/herself and family.

4. *Disclaimable property* The trustee can disclaim property which may be more trouble than it's worth, e.g. unprofitable contracts.

5. *Rights of distress and execution* For example the right of a landlord to distrain (seize and sell) the bankrupt's goods for rent due.

6. *Protected transactions* Probably the single most important area to

have studied thoroughly since it directly involves banks. We consider this next.

Protected transactions

Some protection is needed where a person deals with a debtor in good faith and for valuable consideration in the three months between the first act of bankruptcy and the petition being presented. You *must* know and be able to apply ss.45 and 46 of the 1914 Act.

 Look at Fig. 5.3 which compares the applicability of the two sections. What should appear in the last box?

	Act of bankruptcy	Presentation of petition	Receiving order	Protection
Section 45	No notice	No	Not made	1. 2. 3. 4.
Section 46	Notice irrelevant	No notice	Not made	1.

Fig. 5.3 *Protection under ss.45 and 46*

You can see from the figure that the protection of both sections is lost once the *receiving order* is made, whether or not the person seeking protection had notice of it. In this context you should be able to explain s.4 of the Bankruptcy Amendment Act 1926 and *Re Wigzell* (1921) and *Re Byfield* (1982).

Before we move on, remember that s.47 provides that any dealing in respect of the bankrupt's property after adjudication shall be valid against the trustee provided (i) the other party dealt in good faith and for value, and (ii) the dealing was completed before the trustee intervened to lay claim to the property. In particular, the section specifically provides that a bankrupt's transactions with a banker are dealings for value within its meaning and that for its purposes payments made by the order or direction of a bankrupt are to be deemed transactions by the bankrupt.

Creditors

Here the most important thing is to know and to be able to apply the rules relating to types of creditors:

— secured,
— preferential,
— unsecured,
— deferred.

(We discuss the position of secured and preferential creditors in Topic 4: Companies.)

A small but important point to remember is that s.33 gives no preferential status to a creditor who has advanced money to a debtor to enable him to pay wages, salaries and accrued holiday pay to his employees.

Bankruptcy and banking

As always, you *must* be able to apply the general law to banking. Pay particular attention to the following.

1. *Fraudulent preference* A bank may find itself the party preferred even though the effect is to protect someone else. For example, where the debtor's payments to the bank are intended to reduce or extinguish the liability of a guarantor of his overdraft.

2. *Protected transactions* Until the bank has notice of an act of bankruptcy, s.45 enables a customer's account to be operated normally, even where the bank knows of an intention to commit an act of bankruptcy. *Re Keever v. Midland Bank Ltd* (1967) is a good example of this, the trustee resisting, unsuccessfully, the bank's claim to set-off a cheque against a debit balance.

The question with s.46 is whether or not it protects a banker who pays the debtor's cheques made out to third parties. You should know *Re Dalton* (1962) in this context.

3. *A customer's bankruptcy* More 'practice' than law perhaps, but you should know in outline what action should be taken and why. Sections 45 and 46 apply here — is there notice of an act of bankruptcy, is the account in credit or overdrawn, is it a payment in or a payment out?

The effect of a *receiving order* is simple: the account must be stopped entirely. The balance (if any) on the account and any securities automatically transfer to the Official Receiver or the trustee and must be delivered to him.

An *adjudication order* terminates the contract between the customer and the bank.

4. *A guarantor's bankruptcy* Immediately a bank receives notice that an act of bankruptcy has been committed by or a receiving order made against a person who has guaranteed or deposited securities to secure a customer's overdraft, the customer's account must be stopped to avoid Clayton's Case (1816) operating to the bank's disadvantage. An immediate demand for repayment should then be made to the customer.

Now work through the summary diagram (Fig. 5.4).

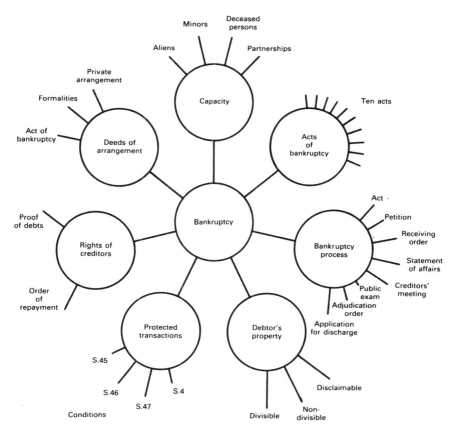

Fig. 5.4

Once you feel confident about your knowledge of this topic, try to answer the 10 multiple choice questions which follow.

Multiple choice questions

1 A debtor is made bankrupt when:

   a   he commits an act of bankruptcy.
   b   a bankruptcy petition is presented against him.
   c   a receiving order is made against him.
   d   an adjudication order is made against him.

2 Which of the following cannot be made bankrupt for rent due for
   lodgings:

   a   an alien?
   b   a seventeen-year old student?
   c   the estate of Mr Smith who died last week?
   d   a partnership?

3 Miss X committed acts of bankruptcy on the following dates:
   (i) 1 March, (ii) 15 March, (iii) 7 May, (iv) 10 June, all in the same
   year. Her account with Mantown Bank was overdrawn during this
   period and unsecured. Having been informed of the act of
   bankruptcy committed on 10 June, the bank presented a petition on
   12 June. Assuming she is adjudicated bankrupt, her trustee's title to
   her property would commence on date:

   a   i.
   b   ii.
   d   iii.
   d   iv.

4 Which of the following types of property is available to the trustee
   for distribution among creditors:

   a   property belonging to the bankrupt as trustee?
   b   a voluntary settlement made 18 months before the first available
       act of bankruptcy?

    c trade tools valued at £225?

    d a right of action in negligence for personal injuries?

5 Fraudulent preferences are defined by the Bankruptcy Act 1914, s.44(1). Which of the following is not a requirement of the section — that the conveyance, transfer or charge was:

    a a voluntary act?

    b committed fraudulently?

    c committed in the 6 months immediately preceding the presentation of the petition?

    d committed when the debtor was insolvent?

6 Which of the following is not a provable debt in the bankruptcy process:

    a unliquidated claims not arising out of a breach of contract?

    b a claim for breach of contract?

    c a contingent debt?

    d an action arising from breach of obligations contained in a trust deed?

7 In the bankruptcy of X, a member of solicitors XYZ & Co, there were the following creditors:

    i   Mantown Bank, holding a legal mortgage on X's house.

    ii   Mantown Builders, claiming payment for alterations to XYZ & Co's offices.

    iii the Professional Car Lease Company.

    iv Miss A, X's articled clerk, for the return of a proportion of the premium she paid to him.

The order of repayment is:

    a i, iv, iii, ii.

    b i, ii, iii, iv.

    c iv, i, iii, ii.

    d iv, ii, i, iii.

8 A deed of arrangement which assigns property to a trustee for the benefit of creditors generally is an act of bankruptcy. Any creditor who does not assent to it may base a bankruptcy petition on it within:

   a 1 month of its execution.
   b 3 months of its execution.
   c 6 months of its execution.
   d 9 months of its execuution.

 *answer*

9 In respect of a customer who is subsequently adjudicated bankrupt, a bank can rely on S.46 of the 1914 Act to:

   a allow the customer to withdraw money from his account when it knows he has committed an act of bankruptcy.
   b allow the customer to withdraw money from his account when it knows a bankruptcy petition has been presented against him.
   c pay a cheque presented by a trade creditor when it knows his customer has committed an act of bankruptcy.
   d pay a cheque presented by a trade creditor when it knows a bankruptcy petition has been presented against its customer.

 *answer*

10 After notice of an act of bankruptcy by a customer, a bank can safely:

   a make payments into the current account.
   b allow the customer to overdraw his account relying on the existence of surplus security held by the bank.
   c pay the customer's third party cheques.
   d deliver safe custody items to the customer.

 *answer*

 Answers follow on pages 88-92. Score 2 marks for each correct answer.

Answers

1 The correct answer is **d**.

If you got this one wrong you don't know your stuff! Go back and revise thoroughly when you've finished going through these answers.

Each of the options is an important stage in the bankruptcy process but it's the adjudication order (answer **d**) which actually makes the debtor bankrupt and vests title to all his available property in his trustee in bankruptcy.

Let's look at the effect of the other answers. Committing one of the 10 acts of bankruptcy (answer **a**) starts the bankruptcy process as each is considered to be an indication that the debtor can't meet his liabilities. A creditor must base his petition on such an act. Remember (i) that the trustee's title dates back to the first act of bankruptcy committed in the three months immediately preceding the presentation of the petition, and (ii) that actual or constructive notice of an act of bankruptcy prevents reliance on s.45.

A petition (answer **b**) must be presented within three months of an act of bankruptcy. Notice of a petition prevents a banker relying on s.46. A receiving order (answer **c**), contrary to popular belief, does not make a debtor bankrupt, although an adjudication order usually follows as a matter of course. The receiving order makes the Official Receiver the receiver of the debtor's property. It must be advertised, registered in relation to land and it prevents the debtor disposing of his property and creditors proceeding individually against him. The making of the receiving order (not notice of it) prevents a banker relying on either s.45 or s.46.

2 The correct answer is **c**.

This question is about capacity in bankruptcy. An alien (answer **a**) is in no special position in bankruptcy law — neither privileges nor disabilities — and can be made bankrupt if:

— he was domiciled in England at the time of committing an act of bankruptcy;
— he was ordinarily resident or had a dwelling house in England within a year before proceedings are commenced;
— He was carrying on business in England;
— he was a member of a firm carrying on business in England.

A seventeen-year-old student (answer **b**) — a minor remember — is only liable for 'necessaries'. Do you remember your contract law?

However, paying for lodgings would be a necessary. Therefore the student would be bound by the contract and bankruptcy proceedings could be taken against him or her if the rent was not paid. A deceased person (answer **c**) cannot be made bankrupt but their estate may be administered in bankruptcy. A partnership (answer **d**) can, of course, be made bankrupt and a receiving order against the firm operates as a receiving order against each person who was a member of the firm at the date of the receiving order.

3 The correct answer is **c**.

This is a common exam question so its worth revising thoroughly. In fact, it's easy to gain high marks on such questions providing you know a simple rule and can explain and apply it to the given facts. You must explain it, otherwise you could be accused of guessing!

The rule concerned is the doctrine of relation back contained in s.37 of the Bankruptcy Act 1914. This states that the commencement of the bankruptcy is the date on which the first available act of bankruptcy was committed within the three months immediately preceding the presentation of the petition. This means that any property which belonged to the debtor that has been transferred since the first available act but which if retained would have been divisible among creditors can be recovered by the trustee from its present owner.

Applying this rule to the facts, the trustee's title dates back three months from 12 June, i.e. to 12 March. Thus, his title to the bankrupt's property begins on 15 March, the act of bankruptcy committed on 1 March being unavailable.

4 The correct answer is **b**.

Answers **a**, **c** and **d** are three examples of non-divisible property — property which is not available for division among creditors. The other examples of non-divisible property are:

— personal earnings necessary to support himself and his family;
— a right of action in defamation;
— the benefit of contracts requiring personal skill;
— old age pensions and other national insurance benefits.

Also remember that the law allows £250 to cover not only tools but also clothing and bedding for himself and his family!

The correct answer — a voluntary settlement — is an example of recoverable property. This is property which the bankrupt was once the owner of, but had transferred before the commencement of his bankruptcy, but which the trustee can nevertheless recover from the transferee. This rule extends the trustee's title beyond the three months available under the doctrine of relation back. The three other situations when property can be recovered in this way are where the bankrupt's transfer of it was a

— fraudulent conveyance,
— fraudulent preference,
— general assignment of book debts.

You should be sure that you thoroughly know the law in relation to fraudulent conveyances and fraudulent preferences.

5 The correct answer is **b**.

Strange though it may seem, fraud in the usual sense of the word, that is 'dishonesty', is not required by the Bankruptcy Act 1914, s.44(1). The other three options are all required. A requirement that you were not given as an option is that the conveyance, transfer or charge was made with intent to prefer. This is the meaning of fraudulent within the section. The final requirement is that the debtor must have been insolvent at the time the preference was made.

6 The correct answer is **a**.

A straightforward question — something you know or you don't know. The best way to approach it is to learn the types of non-provable debts and then all the others must be provable. Non-provable debts are:

— unliquidated damages not arising out of a breach of contract or breach of a trust.
— debts due to any person who knew of an available act of bankruptcy committed by the debtor at the time the debt was incurred.
— debts which in the opinion of the court are incapable of being fairly assessed.
— debts incurred after the date of the receiving order.

A word of explanation about answer **c** — a contingent debt. A contingent debt is one which is dependent on the happening of some future event, e.g. a debt arising after the date of the receiving order through a subsequent breach of an existing contract.

7 The correct answer is **a**.

A common exam question, and one which requires you to explain legal rules and then apply them to the facts. Providing you do just this (correctly!), you'll gain good marks.
The order of repayment of creditors is to:

1. creditors secured by fixed charges;
2. administrative costs and charges incurred in the bankruptcy;
3. pre-preferential debts;
4. preferential creditors;
5. unsecured creditors;
6. deferred creditors.

In the question you were given: a secured creditor (i), a pre-preferential debt (iv), an unsecured creditor (iii), and a deferred creditor (ii). You were not given options involving administration costs and charges incurred in X's bankruptcy or a preferential claim.

8 The correct answer is **b**.

Really a right/wrong question; you must avoid wrongly stating the periods specified by the different bankruptcy rules and processes. If you chose answer **a** (one month) you might have had the Deeds of Arrangement Act 1914, s.24 at the back of your mind. This provides that if the trustee named in the deed of arrangement serves notice of the deed on the creditors, the period in which one or more dissenting creditors can present a petition is reduced to one month.

9 The correct answer is **a**.

Hopefully Fig. 5.3 should have helped you to learn and distinguish between the protection afforded by ss.45 and 46 of the Bankruptcy Act 1914. You will have seen that s.46 affords less protection but extends further into the bankruptcy process. Specifically, it protects any payment of money or delivery of property to a person subsequently adjudicated bankrupt or a person claiming by assignment from him, provided the transaction:

— takes place before the date of the receiving order; and
— without notice of the presentation of a bankrtupcy petition; and
— is either in the ordinary course of business or otherwise *bona fide*.

The fact that the bank knows that its customer has committed an act of bankruptcy in answer **a** is irrelevant to the operation of s.46. However, answer **b** equally clearly fails to satisfy the provisos of s.46, specifically the bank has notice of the presentation of a petition. So that can't be right. Answer **a** also fails to satisfy this requirement as well as being caught up in the same problem as answer **c**. It was suggested in *Re Dalton* (1962) that a banker would be protected by s.46 if he paid the bankrupt's third party cheques (answer **c**). The argument put was that since a banker can safely make payment to the bankrupt who could then pay the money to the third party directly, a payment by a banker direct to the third party on the bankrupt's instructions should be similarly protected. However, it would be better not to rely on this.

10 The correct answer is **d**.

This is an application of s.46, the protection of s.45 being lost by having had notice of the customer's act of bankruptcy.

Before we consider the incorrect answers, remember that delivery of safe custody items (answer **d**) — as well as payments from the account and the delivery of securities — can also be made to a person claiming by assignment from him, e.g. the trustee named in a deed of arrangement.

Payments into the account (answer **a**) are not covered by s.46 and they must be placed in a suspense account for three months in case a petition is presented based on the act of bankruptcy of which the bank has notice. Similarly, payment of third party cheques (answer **c**) are not covered, despite *obiter dicta* in *Re Dalton* (1962), suggesting that they should be.

A payment from the account to the customer which would result in an overdraft (answer **b**) cannot be made because it would be a debt contracted after notice of an act of bankruptcy and such debts are not provable. The existence of surplus security makes no difference because the surplus is subject to the doctrine of relation back.

Score 2 marks for each correct answer. What was your score for this topic? Fill it in on the score grid.

If you scored 12 or less and are still a bit shaky on some points go back and look at the study guide again, before proceeding any further.

If you are sure you really understand and are familiar with the topic now, try the 10 further questions which are on pages 180-183.

Alternatively you can go on to the next topic and do all the post-tests together at the end.

Topic 6   Land and its Use as Security

Study guide

Your syllabus includes both *general land law* and the more specialized law relating to *land's use as security* for lending: you can get questions on either or both aspects. However, you're more likely to be asked questions on land as security because this is far more relevant to you. Questions on the general law tend to be both predictable, e.g. on legal estates, and straightforward. This latter characteristic, in particular, means you have to present a very comprehensive answer to score high marks.

Traditionally, students seem to find everything to do with land law difficult. It's up to you whether or not you think this is so but you'll certainly find land as security far easier to understand and learn if you take the time to really understand *basic terminology* and *principles* of land law. This should be your aim in your revision of the general law.

Estates and interests

Do you understand the difference between an *estate* and an *interest* in land? Be sure that you can explain the words used in the technical legal terminology for the two possible *legal estates* which we know simply as *freehold* and *leasehold*.

— *Fee simple absolute in possession.*
— *Term of years absolute.*

You should not have to waste time thinking about it so write out definitions, if you haven't any, and *learn* them.

From here move on to *interests in land*. Can you distinguish between *legal* and *equitable* interests? Have a go and then check your explanation with your notes or text book. Remember that since 1925 all interests in land other than the *two* legal estates and *five* legal interests exist as *equitable interests only*.

Most interests in land must be *registered* to be protected: registration on the *Proprietorship* or *Charges Register* at the Land Registry if the land is *registered* and on the *Register of Land Charges* if it is not. It is *registration*, not notice of the charge, which protects the holder of the interest.

Title to land

Your life as a student of banking law is made more difficult by there being two co-existing systems of proving and transferring title to land. Land may be *registered* or *unregistered*. Undoubtedly, studying and generally dealing with registered land is easier and, mercifully, title to all land in the country will eventually be registered. You, however, must keep the difference very much in mind; it explains much and avoids some unholy confusion!

Title to *registered land* is proved by entries on a *public register* although the register does not contain an exhaustive list of interests in that particular piece of land: *overriding interests* and some *minor interests* are not shown. You should have an understanding of:

— The division of the register into its *three parts*.
— *Overriding* and *minor interests*.
— The four types of *registered title*.

Title to *unregistered land* is proved by a collection of deeds and documents known as *title deeds*. These must show a chain of title concluding with that of the present owner.

Land as security: what you need to know

In almost every exam paper there's a *full question* on the use of land as security so it's worth revising thoroughly. However, the questions have tended to concentrate on:

— the distinction between *legal and equitable mortgages*, including *remedies*.
— the way in which *equitable mortgages* of both registered and unregistered land can be created.
— the distinction between a *second* and a *sub-mortgage*.
— the *procedure* for taking a *sub-mortgage* and a legal mortgage from a *limited company*.
— a bank's *duties* when *realizing* or *releasing* security.

Legal and equitable mortgages

A *legal mortgage* can be created in two ways, both by deed:

— by a lease to the mortgagee for a term of years, subject to a proviso that the lease will terminate upon repayment of the debt.

— a charge by deed expressed to be by way of legal mortgage.

An *equitable mortgage* can be created by:

— an agreement to create a legal mortgage.
— a deposit of title deeds or land certificate.
— an equitable charge.

Because an equitable mortgage doesn't convey a legal interest in the property, a banker will normally take a *written memorandum of deposit* in which the mortgagor undertakes to execute a legal mortgage as and when called upon to do so.

The basic practical distinction between legal and equitable mortgages concerns the respective bases of remedies available to the mortgagee. A *legal mortgagee* acquires rights against the property itself in addition to the personal action available against the mortgagee for the principal and interest due. An *equitable mortgagee* has no rights against the property, but only personal rights against the borrower.

Bank mortgage forms

It would be unfair to ask you to identify all the usual clauses in a bank's mortgage form but you should be familiar with typical clauses and be able to explain why they are included. If you haven't already got one, obtain a copy of your own bank's legal and equitable mortgage forms and read through their clauses. By referring to your notes or textbook if necessary, work out what each clause does. It will probably take you some time to do this but it will be time well spent. If you make notes in the margins of the forms, you'll have the genuine articles suitably explained to revise from — you can't get more in context than that!

Second and sub-mortgages

 As an exercise, concisely define each and highlight the distinction between them. The ability to recall and explain basic definitions is easily worth three minutes per question!

Taking a bank mortgage

As a banker, you're primarily concerned with three things:

— The *value* of the land offered as security.
— The customer's *title* to it.

95

— The *procedure* to adopt.

Your exam is in banking law, not banking practice, so you can't be expected to know the detail of the procedure. We can summarize this topic in Fig. 6.1.

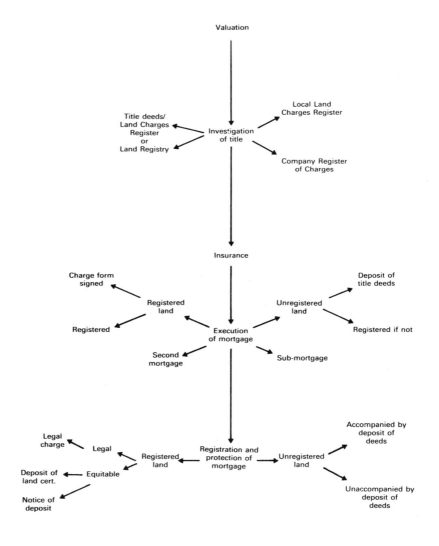

Fig. 6.1 *Taking a bank mortgage*

The mortgagee's remedies

Banks lend money because the lending proposition is acceptable and because the borrower can apparently make repayment, not just because the security offered is adequate. However, should the security have to be relied on there must be no problems or delays in realizing it. A bank mortgage form is designed to ensure this. It will make available all possible remedies and exclude certain provisions of the Law of Prooperty Act 1925 which, if not excluded, would delay the realization.

A *legal mortgagee's* remedies are superior to those of an equitable mortgagee. As you have seen, he has rights against the land itself (*rights in rem*) while an *equitable mortgagee* only has rights against the mortgagor (*rights in personam*). An equitable mortgagee can't take action against the mortgaged property itself without the court's sanction and help.

Legal mortgagee Write down the *five* remedies that are available. Note which are the more commonly used remedies.
Equitable mortgagee The remedies will be detailed in the *memorandum of deposit*. Write down what they will include.

The number you list will depend on your notes/textbook.

You already know that an *equitable mortgagee* does not enjoy rights against the mortgaged property as such. However, he can put himself in much the same position as a legal mortgagee by the simple expedient of taking the *mortgage under seal* (*by deed*) because the Law of Property Act 1925, s.101 provides that any mortgage under seal gives the mortgagee the power of sale and the power to appoint a receiver, the two most useful remedies to a banker. Furthermore, and this is a good example of a bank using the law to protect its interests, its equitable mortgage under seal will always include a power of attorney or a declaration of trust with the power to replace the mortgagor as trustee. This means it can convey the legal estate to the purchaser, if it has to sell the property, without recourse to the court.

Redemption and discharge of mortgages

Here you should be able to:

— Explain the *equity of redemption* and how it cannot be '*clogged*'.
— Outline the *procedure* for discharging a bank mortgage, distinguishing between legal and equitable mortgages, and registered and unregistered land.

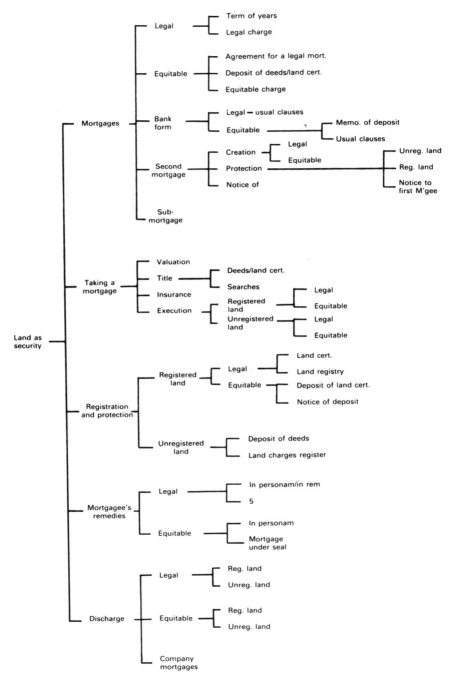

Fig. 6.2 *Land as security*

One more topic studied — well done! On to the summary diagram (Fig. 6.2). Since this is such a large subject, we're just summarizing 'Land as Security' in the diagram. You could usefully draw a diagram of the general law using your own notes or our Study Guide as your raw material.

Once you feel confident about your knowledge of this topic, try to answer the 10 multiple choice questions which follow.

Multiple choice questions

1 Real property is:

 a   all land.
 b   all freehold land.
 c   all leasehold land.
 d   all land with buildings on it.

2 A legal assignment of a lease:

 a   can be effected orally.
 b   can be effected by a written document.
 c   must be evidenced by a note or memorandum in writing.
 d   must be effected by deed.

3 Overriding interests bind a purchaser of the land to which they relate:

 a   if he has notice of them.
 b   if they are registered under the Land Charges Act 1972.
 c   if they are registered at the Land Registry.
 d   whether or not they are registered.

4 *Williams & Glyn's Bank Ltd v. Boland* (1980) established that a wife who contributes to the purchase of a matrimonial home and who is in actual occupation:

 a   must register her interest as a Class F charge.
 b   acquires a minor interest which must be protected by entry of a notice on the Charges Register.
 c   acquires an overriding interest which must be registered on the Charges Register.
 d   acquires an overriding interest which does not require registration.

5   When a receiving order is made against a person who owns registered land, a bankruptcy inhibition is entered on the:

   a   Register of Writs and Orders affecting land.
   b   Property Register.
   c   Proprietorship Register.
   d   Charges Register.

6   A sub-mortgage is created when:

   a   an additional mortgage is created over a property already mortgaged.
   b   a mortgagee mortgages an existing mortgage debt.
   c   a mortgagee exercises his right to consolidate two or more mortgages.
   d   a mortgagee tacks subsequent advances onto the initial advance.

7   When a bank holding a first mortgage receives notice of a second mortgage, the notice:

   a   prevents the bank taking a third mortgage over the property.
   b   terminates the first mortgage as a continuing security.
   c   prevents the bank exercising its rights under the Law of Property Act 1925, s.94.
   d   removes any exclusion of the Law of Property Act 1925, s.93 contained in the first mortgage.

8   Which of the following remedies is available to both legal and equitable mortgagees without recourse to the court:

   a   an action for the debt?
   b   sale of the property?
   c   appointment of a receiver?
   d   foreclosure?

9 *Cuckmere Brick Co Ltd v. Mutual Finance Ltd* (1971) established that a mortgagee exercising his power of sale:

  a acts as a trustee for the mortgagor.

  b is trustee of the proceeds of the sale.

  c is under a duty to take reasonable care to obtain the true value of the property.

  d does not have to wait for an improvement in the relevant property market.

 answer

10 Which of the following remedies of a mortgagee is designed primarily to recover interest due on a loan rather than primarily to recover the principal sum and put an end to the security:

  a sale?

  b an action for the debt?

  c appointing a receiver?

  d foreclosure?

 answer

Answers follow on pages 103-106. Score 2 marks for each correct answer.

Answers

1 The correct answer is **b**.

If you got this one wrong it probably means that you need to spend an hour or so revising to understand some basic things about land law. Leasehold land, for historical reasons, is classed as personal property. Thus answers **a** and **c** can't be right.

At law, land includes any permanent structure on it and when houses are advertised for sale it is usual to refer to the house as being freehold or leasehold rather than to the land itself. So, if **d** had read 'any freehold land . . .' this too would have been correct. However, it referred to all land and, as you've just seen, leasehold land is personal property.

2 The correct answer is **d**.

Perhaps we should start by considering the creation of a lease. A legal term of years (leasehold) — as opposed to an equitable term — for a period of up to three years can be created orally or in writing, provided it takes effect immediately and at the best rent which can reasonably be obtained. A lease for more than three years must be granted by deed to create a legal estate. A legal assignment of a lease, no matter how short the term and no matter how created, must be effected by deed.

A word about answer **c**. If you selected this answer you were probably thinking of the Law of Property Act 1925, s.40 which requires a contract for the sale of land to be actually in writing or provable by written evidence.

3 The correct answer is **d**.

Quite a lot is involved in this question. Overriding interests are interests which could be discovered from enquiries of the occupier or by an inspection of the land itself, and not (if title to the land were unregistered) from the title deeds and documents relating to the land, e.g. an easement such as a right of way.

The first point to make on the answers is that overriding interests belong to the system of registered land. The Land Charges Act 1972 is part of the system of unregistered land so answer **b** has nothing at all to do with overriding interests. The second point is that the doctrine of notice was superseded by the process of registering interests by the Land Charges Act 1925 (unregistered land) and the Land Registration Act 1925 (registered land). Overriding interests are, in fact, effective whether or not the purchaser (the term includes a mortgagee) has notice of them. Answer **a** is incorrect therefore.

The third point is that while the Land Registry would be the appropriate place to register overriding interests they bind the purchaser of registered land even though he has no notice of them and they are not mentioned on the register. Hence answer **d** is right and answer **c** wrong. For the record, the Registrar is only under an obligation to enter a notice of the existence of an overriding interest created by a instrument which appears on the title at the time of first registration.

4 The correct answer is **d**.

A decision of considerable significance to banks, and one you must know and be able to apply in problem questions. You've just seen in the previous answer that overriding interests don't have to be registered. So, if a bank wants to make certain that no overriding interests exist over the security offered, it must make suitable enquiries of the occupier and inspect the land. (Does your own bank do this?)

A spouse, of course, does have an interest in the matrimonial home. If the land is registered it is a minor interest and must be protected by registering a notice on the Charges Register (answer **b**). If the land is unregistered, the interest must be registered as a Class F Charge (answer **a**). However, this is laid down by the relevant statutes and wasn't decided by the case. In fact, *Boland's Case* protects a spouse where his or her interest is not registered and the principle clearly applies to anybody who can establish a financial stake in the property and who is in actual occupation. Once again, a decision you must know; you'll find a good account and explanation of it in

Cases in Banking Law: Gheerbrant: Macdonald & Evans.

5 The correct answer is **c**.

Did you read the question carefully? It specified registered land. Really a right or wrong question.

A receiving order is made against the proprietor and not the land itself so it's logical that it should be entered on the Proprietorship Register. The Register of Writs and Orders affecting land (answer **a**) can't be right because this is a register kept under the Land Charges Act 1972 and applies exclusively to unregistered land.

6 The correct answer is **b**.

Perhaps not very common but a sub-mortgage is a good security because of its three-fold nature. To the personal obligation of the sub-mortgagor (the bank's customer) is added the personal obligation of the original mortgagor which is supported by rights against the land itself. It's still quite a mouthful to explain, however. Answer **a** is the definition of a second mortgage.

Answers **c** and **d** are nothing to do with sub-mortgages but are worth short explanations. Consolidation (answer **c**) prevents the mortgagor from redeeming a valuable mortgage while unsatisfactory ones are left outstanding. A bank can thereby prevent the mortgagor redeeming one mortgage in advance of others. Banks give themselves this right in their mortgages by a clause excluding s.93 of the Law of Property Act 1925. Tacking (answer **d**) is the term used where a mortgagee under an obligation to make further advances (a bank financing a building scheme for example) is able to add such advances on to the original advance in priority to a second and subsequent mortgagees.

7 The correct answer is **b**.

Property is often mortgaged more than once at any one time. Any householder, for example, with a property worth substantially more than the outstanding mortgage debt has a security just sitting there waiting to be utilized.

There's nothing legally to prevent a bank taking a third mortgage over the property (answer **a**). It would of course rank in priority after the first and second, but providing there was sufficient equity in the property there should be few if any problems in practice.

Answer **c** concerns tacking — which we mentioned in the previous answer. The right to tack further advances on to the original advance in priority to a second mortgage only applies, as you've seen, to a mortgagee under an obligation to make further advances. Receiving notice of a second mortgage does not affect this right. If the mortgagee is not under such an obligation, the notice does, however, prevent him making further advances which have priority over the second mortgage.

Section 93 of the Law of Property Act 1925 (answer **d**) prevents a mortgagee consolidating mortgages unless it is expressly excluded. Notice of a second mortgage is irrelevant here.

The really important effect of the right answer (terminating the first mortgage as a continuing security) is that the customer's account must be broken to prevent *Clayton's Case* (1816) working to the bank's detriment. Be sure that you can state the rule without having to think about it. You're almost bound to be asked a question which involves the rule in some way.

8 The correct answer is **a**.

A legal mortgagee has both rights *in personam* (rights against the mortgagor) and rights *in rem* (rights against the mortgaged property). An equitable mortgagee has only rights against the mortgagor. The only personal remedy in the options given to you was an action for the debt. Nevertheless, a bank's equitable mortgage will give it the right to apply to the court to exercise the remedies which would be its as of right if it held a legal mortgage. You must also remember that where an equitable mortgage is taken by deed, the mortgagee has the power to sell the property or to appoint a receiver, i.e. rights *in rem*, by virtue of the Law of Property Act 1925, s.101.

9 The correct answer is **c**.

Another important decision. In the case it was specifically held that the mortgagee does not act as trustee for the mortgagor (answer **a**) when he sells the property. Thus, while he is under a duty to try to obtain the best price he can (answer **c**) he is entitled to look to his own interests if they conflict with those of the mortgagor. The fact that he does not have to wait for an improvement in the relevant property market (answer **d**) is specifically the *ratio* in a later case: *Bank of Cyprus (London) v. Gill* (1979).

The mortgagee is indeed the trustee of the proceeds of the sale for the mortgagor but *Cuckmere's Case* (1971) didn't establish this.

10 The correct answer is **c**.

Banks are not in the business of putting customers out of business or out of their homes unless there is no alternative. If there is reasonable hope that within an acceptable time the mortgagor will once again be able to meet his commitments under the mortgage, they will prefer to wait for capital repayment while ensuring they continue to receive the interest due. In the case of business property this can be done by appointing a receiver or by taking possession (directly or constructively). Either remedy enables the bank to receive any income arising from the property. For practical reasons, taking possession is unusual.

The other three remedies given to you as options are used to recover the principal sum due and, in the case of **a** (sale) and **d** (forclosure) terminate the security.

Score 2 marks for each correct answer. What was your score for this topic? Fill it in on the score grid.

If you scored 12 or less and are still a bit shaky on some points go back and look at the study guide again, before proceeding with the post-test.

If you are sure you really understand and are familiar with the topic now, try the 10 further questions which are on pages 183-185.

Alternatively you can go on to the next topic and do all the post-tests together at the end.

Topic 7   Life Assurance Policies and Stock and Shares

Study guide

We've chosen to combine life assurance policies and stocks and shares in one topic because they are both comparatively short and straight-forward. It's also usual only to be set half a question on each and they are sometimes combined in one question.

Life assurance policies

Introduction

Although you're far more likely to be set questions on the use of life assurance policies *as security*, you could be asked to explain one or more basic points about them. In addition, as we've emphasized on several occasions, it's important that you at least *understand* the relevant basic principles. So, you should be able to explain the following — make short concise notes if you haven't got them already.

1   *Types* of life assurance policy, particularly the differences between whole life and endowment, and policies covered by the Married Woman's Property Act 1882.

2   The nature of an *insurable interest*. Be able to give examples.

3   The principle of *uberrima fides*. What is a material fact? *Woolcott v. Sun Alliance and London Insurance Ltd* (1978) is a good case to know on this point.

4   The effect of *suicide* on the policy and hence its value as security.

5   *Assignment* of a life policy, the assignment transferring the right to claim under the policy from the policyholder to another person (the assignee). Remember that the assignee, e.g. a bank, does *not* have to have an insurable interest in the life assured. The Policies of Assurance Act 1867 requires an assignment to be either an indorsement of the policy itself or by a separate document of assignment in the form laid down by the Act. Section 1 gives the assignee the right to sue on the policy in *his own name* provided *notice in writing of the assignment* is given to the issuing company. The assignee also takes *subject to equities*, meaning, for example,

that if the policy could be avoided by the company on the grounds that the proposer failed to disclose a material fact, the assignee will not be able to claim on the policy. All in all, the Act is very important to a bank's position as an assignee of policies for security purposes.

Life policies as security

1 A *legal mortgage* of a life policy is taken by an *assignment under seal*. Remember that if the policy is one to which the Married Women's Property Act 1882 applies, all the beneficiaries named in the policy must be party to the assignment. If all the beneficiaries are not identified with reasonable certainty, or if any are under 18 years of age, no effective charge can be taken.

2 An *equitable mortgage* is taken by a deposit of the policy, usually supported by a memorandum of deposit setting out the terms of the mortgage and the rights of the bank as mortgagee. A bank will give notice of the equitable mortgage to the life assurance company.

3 The *remedies* of a mortgagee of a life policy depend upon whether the policy moneys have become payable or not and on whether the mortgage is legal or equitable. A *legal mortgagee* of a policy which has become payable is entitled to the policy moneys. If they are not payable, he has the following four remedies:

— *surrender* of the policy;
— raising a *loan* against the policy — the policy holder must make the application to the company;
— *sale* of the policy;
— conversion of the policy into a *paid-up policy* for a smaller capital sum.

An *equitable mortgagee* does not hold title to the policy and if the policy moneys have become payable, the mortgagor, or his personal representatives if he has died, must join with the bank in a receipt for the policy moneys. If the moneys are not payable, the mortgagee can:

— Ask the mortgager to *execute a legal assignment* of the policy. The mortgagor will have undertaken to do this in the memorandum of deposit. This enables the bank to exercise the rights of a legal mortgagee listed above.
— Seek the *mortgagor's agreement to the sale or surrender* of the policy.
— Seek the *mortgagor's aid in converting the policy into a paid-up policy* or in obtaining a *loan* from the issuing company.

You will see as you revise other 'security' topics that the rights of legal and equitable mortgagees are the same or similar — in particular, that a legal mortgagor can exercise his remedies as of right while an equitable mortgagee must enlist the help of the mortgagor or the court. One final point before we turn to the discharge of mortgages. If *notice of a subsequent charge* of the policy is received, an unlikely occurrence admittedly since the bank will invariably have possession of the policy, the mortgagor's account must be broken to prevent the Rule in *Clayton's Case* (1816) working to the bank's detriment. As we've said in the Study Guides to other topics, you *must* be able to explain and, if necessary, illustrate the working of the Rule without having to pause for thought.

4 A *legal mortgage* of a life policy is discharged by a *re-assignment under seal*, notice of the re-assignment being given to the issuing company. An *equitable mortgage* is discharged by cancelling the memorandum of deposit and giving notice of this to the company.

5 *Advantages and disadvantages*: a question on 'securities', be they 'land', 'life policies', 'stocks and shares' or 'guarantees', could require a discussion of their relative strengths and weaknesses as security. Be sure you have clear notes identifying the major strengths and weaknesses of each.

Stocks and shares

As with life policies, you're far more likely to be set questions on the use of stocks and shares as security than on the nature of the various types. However, you must know the difference between *registered* and *bearer* securities and appreciate that 'stocks and shares' is here being used as an umbrella term.

Title to *registered* securities is proved by an entry on a register maintained by the company or other organization issuing the securities. A certificate is issued to the holder and this is *prima facie* evidence of title. Title is transferred by lodging the appropriate transfer form signed by the transferor (and sometimes the transfereee) and the relevant certificate with the issuing organization for appropriate entries to be made on the register. The transferee is then issued with a new certificate. Remember that National Savings Securities and some building society shares are not transferable.

Bearer securities are negotiable instruments and therefore the person in possession of them is *prima facie* the owner of them. You should know from your studies of the subject that title to bearer negotiable instruments is transferred by mere *delivery* and that a person who takes a transfer in good faith and for value acquires a good title, even though the person transferring them had either a defective title or no title at all. This characteristic makes them ideal for security purposes. Be able to explain how American and Canadian share certificates differ from fully negotiable securities.

Stocks and shares as security

The use of stocks and shares *as security* is what you must learn thoroughly, particularly equitable mortgages, because these are far more often encountered than legal mortgages.

1 An *equitable mortgage* of registered stocks and shares is created by a *deposit* of the share certificates, although it is standard practice to also take a *memorandum of deposit*. What are the usual clauses in the memorandum? You're not likely to be asked to list them but if presented with one or more of them you must be able to explain their purpose. Obtain a copy of your own bank's memorandum of deposit and read it through carefully considering the effect of each clause. What is a *blank transfer* and why is it taken? It's important that you know this.

2 A *legal mortgage* of registered stocks and shares is effected by transferring legal title to the shares to the bank or, more usually, its nominee company. But why are equitable mortgages far more usual? Well, it's basically because a legal mortgage makes the bank the actual owner of the shares and administrative costs of one kind or another are bound to be incurred dealing with the usual communications between a company and its shareholders. An equitable mortgage supported by a memorandum of deposit and a blank transfer is usually considered to be sufficient security and avoids such problems. However, questions have involved a more detailed look at the relative strengths and weaknesses of legal and equitable mortgages and this is a topic you could prepare more thoroughly.

3 Bearer securities are not mortgaged but *pledged*. Remember, as negotiable instruments their deposit alone is sufficient to transfer title to them. A banker will usually, however, take a memorandum of deposit because this will set out its rights in the transaction. Unless a bank is aware of circumstances which warrant investigation, it's not under a duty to enquire into the pledgor's title to the securities: *London Joint Stock Bank v. Simmons* (1892).

4 If a bank has to *rely* on the security, a legal mortgage of registered securities together with the memorandum of deposit gives it the right to sell them. An equitable mortgage gives no right of sale itself but the memorandum will contain the mortgagor's undertaking to effect a legal mortgage when asked to do so, which does. Taking a blank transfer (see above) confers an implied power of sale on the bank, exercisable after reasonable notice to the borrower, and a memorandum of deposit taken in addition confers an express power of sale. The memorandum taken with a deposit of bearer securities will confer an express power of sale on the bank.

5 A legal mortgage of registered securities is *discharged* by re-transferring the shares to the mortgagor, an equitable mortgage by returning the certificates, cancelling the memorandum of deposit and, if taken, the blank transfer. A pledge of bearer securities is discharged by cancelling the memorandum if deposit.

6 Finally, could you answer a question comparing the relative strengths and weaknesses of legal and equitable mortgages of stocks and shares and, generally, their advantages and disadvantages as banking securities?

Now work through the summary diagrams in Figs 7.1 and 7.2.

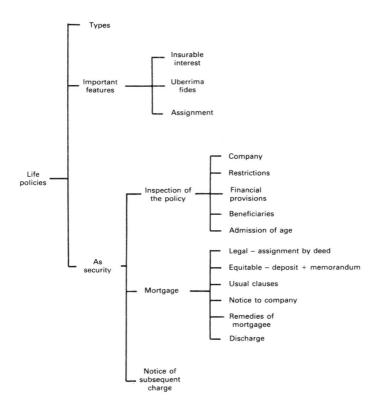

Fig. 7.1 *Life policies*

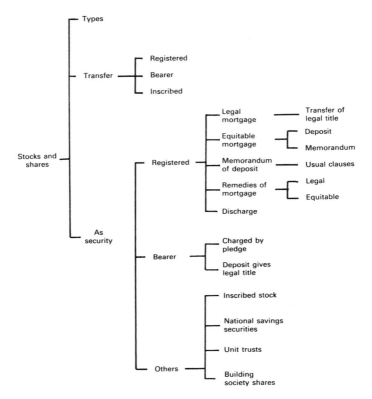

Fig.7.2 *Stocks and shares*

Once you feel confident about your knowledge of this topic, try to answer the 10 multiple choice questions which follow.

Multiple choice questions

1 Which of the following types of policy is intended to mature during the lifetime of the policyholder:

  a   whole life?
  b   endowment?
  c   with profits?
  d   policies under the Married Women's Property Act 1882, s.11.

 answer

2 To transfer legal title, an assignment of a life policy must be:

  a   by an indorsement of the policy itself.
  b   by deed.
  c   to a person with an insurable interest in the life assured.
  d   notified to the issuing company.

 answer

3 A policy to which the Married Women's Property Act 1882, s.11 applies can

  a   never be used a security.
  b   only be used as security if the beneficiaries are named in the policy.
  c   only be used as security if the beneficiaries are named in the policy and join in the assignment.
  d   only be used as security if the beneficiaries are named in the policy, join in the assignment and sign a free will clause.

 answer

4 A banker will take a legal mortgage of a life policy by:

  a   a deposit of the policy.
  b   a deposit of the policy plus a memorandum of deposit.
  c   an indorsement of the policy.
  d   a separate deed of assignment.

 answer

5 A banker's memorandum of deposit taken with a legal mortgage of a life policy will exclude the Law of Property Act 1925, s.103 in order to:

a make the mortgage a continuing security.
b secure all moneys owing.
c enable the bank to demand repayment at any time.
d enable the bank to exercise its right to sell the property immediately a demand for repayment is not satisfied.

6 Title to registered securities is transferred:

a by delivery and indorsement of the securities.
b by completion of a 'Talisman' transfer form.
c by appropriate entries on the register.
d when a new certificate is issued to the transferee.

7 Which of the following clauses would only be found in a memorandum of deposit taken with a equitable mortgage of registered securities:

a an all moneys clause?
b a clause making it a continuing security?
c a specified margin of cover clause?
d a clause in which the mortgagor undertakes to deliver all bonus and rights issues received to the bank?

8 An equitable mortgage of stocks and shares is created by:

a their deposit with the bank.
b their deposit with the bank supported by a memorandum of deposit.
c their deposit with the bank supported by a blank transfer form.
d their deposit with the bank supported by a memorandum of deposit and a blank transfer form.

9 A mortgage of registered securities only has an express power of sale over them if:

a he is registered as the holder of the securities.

b the law of Property Act 1925, s.103 is excluded.

c a memorandum of deposit is taken to support the deposit of the securities.

d notice of lien was sent to the company when the mortgage was taken.

 *answer*

10 All things being equal, which of the following would be the best security:

a a legal mortgage of bearer securities?

b a legal mortgage of registered securities issued by a public company?

c a legal mortgage of registered securities issued by a private company?

d a legal mortgage of National Savings Certificates?

 *answer*

 Answers follow on pages 116-120. Score 2 marks for each correct answer.

115

Answers

1 The correct answer is **b**.

It's unlikely that you would be asked a question involving a discussion of types of life policies as such but you should know the differences between the main kinds. A whole life policy (answer **a**) matures only on the death of the life assured; in other words, the term of the policy is not fixed. An endowment policy (answer **b**) on the other hand is for a specified number of years, often 20 or 25, is frequently taken out these days to secure a mortgage, and is often viewed as an investment as well as a means of ensuring that dependants are provided for should the unthinkable happen.

Both whole life and endowment policies can be 'with profits' policies (answer **c**). Such policies share in the profits of the issuing company. Policies under the Married Women's Property Act 1882 (answer **d**) can in turn be either whole life or endowment, with profits or without profits. Such policies are those where one spouse assures his life for the benefit of the other spouse or their children. A trust is created in favour of the person(s) named in the policy. What you must remember about them is that when one is offered as security, all the beneficiaries must consent to the charge.

2 The correct answer is **d**.

In fact the notice (answer **d**) must be in writing: Policies of Assurance Act 1867, s.3. Section 5 provides that an assignment of life policy must be made in one of two ways: by an indorsement of the policy itself (answer **a**) or by a separate document of assignment in the form laid down by the Act. Banks will take an assignment by deed (answer **b**) in this form. However, neither answer **a** nor **b** is absolutely correct because, as you've just seen, the 1867 Act does allow a choice in the method of assignment. Banks choose to use a deed. Notice in writing (answer **d**) must always be given.

An assignee is not required to have an insurable interest (answer **c**) in the life assured: Life Assurance Act 1774, s.1.

3 The correct answer is **c**.

You've seen in question 1 that a policy under the Married Women's Property Act 1882, s.11 creates a trust in favour of the beneficiaries named in the policy. In other words, they have an equitable interest of which a bank taking the policy has notice. The bank's interest as mortgagee would therefore be subject to it. Hence, in order to make the policy an acceptable security, the beneficiaries must assign their interests to the bank by joining in the assignment of the policy by the policy holder (answer **c**). You must also remember that if all possible beneficiaries are not identified with reasonable certainty, or if any are under 18 years of age, no effective charge can be taken.

If answer **c** is right (which it is), it follows that answers **a** and **b** can't be right. A word about answer **d**. When a bank takes a charge of such a policy, it will usually insist that the beneficiaries sign a free will clause to the effect that they have had the consequences of joining the assignment fully explained to them by a competent, independent third party, e.g. a solicitor. Such a clause should prevent one of the beneficiaries from subsequently pleading that he can avoid the assignment on the grounds of undue influence. Clearly, free will clauses are important but they are not an actual condition of the use of policies under s.11 as security. And that's what the question asked.

4 The correct answer is **d**.

A straightforward question — you shouldn't have got it wrong. Answers **a** and **b** both apply to equitable mortgages of life policies. The mere deposit of a life policy creates an equitable mortgage in the bank's favour but a bank will almost invariably take a memorandum of deposit as well because it can then specify in it the purpose of the deposit, the terms of the mortgage and its rights as mortgagee.

Under the Policies of Assurance Act 1867, s.5 an assignment of a life policy can be by an indorsement on the policy itself (answer **c**) but banks will not take a mortgage by such an assignment. You were specifically asked how a bank would take a legal mortgage. They do it by a separate deed of assignment (answer **d**).

5 The correct answer is **d**.

A right/wrong question, something you either knew or you didn't. The memorandum of deposit taken with a legal mortgage of a life policy will indeed make the mortgage a continuing security (answer **a**) and ensure that it covers all moneys owing at any time on any account (answer **b**) but s.103 has nothing to do with these. If it was not excluded, s.103 would prevent the bank exercising its power of sale until three months had elapsed since the demand for repayment was made.

A clause making the advance secured repayable on demand (answer **c**) is included because of the Limitation Act 1980. Without the clause, the limitation period of six years would begin running from the date on which the mortgage was created, not what a banker wants in a long-term security. The clause makes the limitation period run from the time a demand for repayment is made.

6   The correct answer is **c**.

We can dispense with answer **a** quickly. If you chose this answer you were probably thinking about bearer securities but even here the statement is incorrect. Bearer securities do not need to be indorsed to transfer title to them — delivery alone is sufficient. Completion of a 'Talisman' transfer form (answer **b**), a variant of the stock transfer form and introduced with computer accounting in the Stock Exchange, does not itself transfer title. It's merely the means by which the information that the company requires to effect a transfer is presented to the company. Evidence of title is the register itself so transfer of title must be effected by entries on the same register (answer **c**). The new certificate issued (answer **d**) is merely *prima facie* evidence of title. As such, however, its deposit with a bank creates an equitable mortgage.

7   The correct answer is **d**.

Answers **a**, **b** and **c** are all important clauses found in memoranda of deposit taken to support both legal and equitable mortgages. The all moneys clause (answer **a**) ensures, as you've already seen, that the mortgage covers all liabilities which may be owed to the bank at any time and on any account. Furthermore, interest and commission payments and any expenses incurred by the bank in taking and enforcing the security are included. The continuing security clause is included to ensure that the mortgage covers the outstanding balance at any given time. This avoids the Rule in *Clayton's Case* (1816) operating to the bank's detriment. (Can you explain the Rule without hesitation?)

Under the specified margin of cover clause (answer **c**) the customer undertakes to maintain the value of the shares deposited at a given value above that of the advance secured. This should ensure that the bank is not adversely affected by a sudden drop in value of the shares. Answer **d**, the correct answer — an undertaking to deliver all bonus and rights issued received to the bank — is included only in an equitable mortgage because the mortgagor is still the legal owner of the shares and all such issues will be addressed to him or her. If the mortgagor takes advantage of this for his own purposes, the value of the security held by the bank will be reduced. Another clause only found in an equitable mortgage is one under which the mortgagor undertakes to complete on request any formalities necessary to perfect the bank's title to the securities.

8   The correct answer is **a**.

The mere deposit of stocks and shares is sufficient to create an equitable mortgage over them (answer **a**). So, all the other answers are 'legally' wrong. However, had the question asked how a bank took an equitable mortgage of stocks and shares, these other answers could all have been correct. Banking practice frequently modifies basic legal rules, particularly where the bank's own position is strengthened by so doing. This is a good example.

Taking a memorandum of deposit (answer **b**) enables the bank to detail the terms of the mortgage, in particular its rights and remedies.

Taking a blank transfer form (answer **c**) with a deposit of the certificates enables a bank to transfer legal ownership of the securities to itself or, more usually, its nominee company, by inserting its name as transferee and registering the transfer whenever it considers it advisable to do so. Alternatively the transfer may be completed in favour of a purchaser if the bank exercises its power of sale under the mortgage.

Taking both a memorandum of deposit and a blank transfer (answer **d**) puts the bank in almost as strong a position as equitable mortgagee as it would be if it held a legal mortgage. The blank transfer gives the bank an implied power of sale which becomes an express power, i.e. as of right, if a memorandum of deposit is also taken.

9   The correct answer is **c**.

Registration as holder of the securities (answer **a**) is what transfers legal title to stocks and shares but it is the taking of a memorandum of deposit (answer **c**) from the customer which contains the power of sale. The Law of Property Act 1925, s.103 (answer **b**) does deal with the power of sale but requires that a minimum period of three months must elapse between the demand for repayment and the exercise of the power. As you've seen, s.103 is invariably excluded in bank mortgage forms, thereby giving the bank the right to sell the security immediately a demand for repayment is not met or, at worst, after a short period of notice, usually one month.

Notice of lien (answer **d**) is nothing to do with the power of sale. Giving notice of lien is one of two ways in which an equitable mortgagee of stocks and shares can partially protect his position. The other method is by notice in lieu of distingras.

10   The correct answer is **a**.

Bearer securities (answer **a**) would be the best security, all things being equal, because (i) title to bearer securities is transferred by mere delivery and (ii) as a result very little formality and expense is incurred in taking the security. The other securities would rank in the order **b**, **c**, **d**. Shares in private companies can be difficult to value because they are not quoted on the Stock Exchange and the company's articles of association may affect their value as security, e.g. their transferability may be restricted which would mean that they would be harder to sell. National Savings Certificates are not transferable and therefore only an equitable mortgage of them is possible.

Score 2 marks for each correct answer. What was your score for this topic? Fill it in on the score grid.

If you scored 12 or less and are still a bit shaky on some points go back and look at the study guide again, before proceeding any further.

If you are sure you really understand and are familiar with the topic now, try the 10 further questions which are on pages 185-187.

Alternatively you can go on to the next topic and do all the post-tests together at the end.

Topic 8 Guarantees

Study guide

Guarantees in perspective

This is a compact, straightforward topic for you to study. Guarantees are also a very straightforward security to take and realize. Interestingly enough, though, it's banking practice, particularly the lengthy guarantee forms banks use, which make it straightforward rather than the law itself, for this can be complicated. In fact, bank guarantee forms are an excellent example of an organization using standard form contracts to maximize the strength of its own position against that of the other. In other words, bank guarantee forms *exclude* virtually all the guarantor's (or surety's) common law rights. It's small wonder that something so one-sided (but, we hasten to add, perfectly legitimate and proper) is straightforward; there's rarely room for dispute!

What should I learn?

For the purposes of your revision, the topic falls into two neat parts: the general *legal framework* and then *bank guarantees*. You can get questions on either but it's far more likely that a question will be set on:

— The *usual clauses* in a bank guarantee form — you'll most likely be given them and asked to explain their purpose and effect.
— *Problems* involving a general knowledge and application of the usual clauses — particularly, perhaps, dealing with situations involving undue influence and misrepresentation.
— Special *types* of guarantees, e.g. those given by co-guarantors or by companies.

The legal framework

Definition

A guarantee is a promise to answer 'for the debt, default or miscarriage of another' if that person fails to meet his obligation: Statute of Frauds

1677, s.4. Looking at this definition you can see that it includes things other than debts — the performance of a contract, for example — but for our purposes it's *debts* which are relevant.

Main features

There are five:

- *Three parties* are involved (creditor, debtor and guarantor) and *two contracts*.
- A *valid debt must exist* between the creditor and debtor.
- The guarantor incurs *secondary liability*, i.e. he becomes liable *only if* the debtor fails to pay.
- The guarantor has *no direct interest* in the contract between the debtor and creditor.
- There must be *written evidence* of a guarantee and its terms for it to be enforceable at law: Statute of Frauds 1677, s.4.

Guarantees and indemnities

A basic point perhaps, but be sure you know the difference. You've just seen that a guarantor incurs secondary liability but an indemnifier incurs primary liability, i.e. he is liable to pay whatever happens. Remember that a bank guarantee form will include an *ultra vires* clause whenever there is a possibility that the original debt may prove invalid. This has the effect of converting the guarantee into an indemnity should this happen. A practical point, of course, is that no written evidence of an indemnity is required to be able to enforce it.

Legal capacity

First the *principal debtor*: he or she must be capable of incurring the debt guaranteed. You can't guarantee something which legally doesn't exist! This is where an *ultra vires* clause is important, but remember *Coutts & Co v. Browne-Lecky* (1947). Similarly, the guarantor must have the legal capacity to give the guarantee. Be sure that you know the special rules relating to:

- co-guarantors,
- partners,
- companies.

Reality of consent

Here two topics must be understood: misrepresentation and undue influence. *Misrepresentation* by the creditor always entitles the guarantor to avoid the guarantee; this common law right can't be excluded by the guarantee form. *Undue influence* is perhaps more complex and subtle. When does a presumption of undue influence exist? What are 'free will' and 'attestation' clauses? Make a quick note in the margin if you don't know. Two cases you ought to know here are our old friend *Lloyds Bank v. Bundy* (1975) and *National Westminster Bank plc v. Morgan* (1985).

A third topic should also be included here perhaps. The possibility that the surety could plead *non est factum*, i.e., that he or she was completely mistaken about the nature of the contract signed. However, this is an extremely unlikely plea because a bank will ensure that a would-be surety receives independent advice where there is doubt about his or her understanding of the nature of the agreement or its implications and it will invariably be signed at the bank or in the presence of the independent adviser. *Saunders v. Anglia Building Society* (1970) was the decision which marked the effective disappearance of such a plea.

Disclosure of information

A guarantee is *not* a contract *uberrimae fidei*; this is your starting point here. Therefore, a bank doesn't have to disclose to the surety everything it knows that may be relevant to the agreement — it's up to the surety to ask. One specific point you should know here is how far a surety is entitled to know the extent of his liability under the guarantee. The Consumer Credit Act 1974 is relevant here, remember.

Bank guarantees

The first thing you should do, if you haven't already done so, is to obtain a copy of your own bank's guarantee form. As you revise the various clauses, find them in the form and, perhaps, make the odd note or two in the margin. There's nothing like reality to help you to understand and learn something.

What do they do?

Obviously, they fulfil the requirements of the general legal framework but in particular they will:

— state the *liability* of the surety;
— prevent the Rule in *Clayton's Case* (1816) operating to the bank's detriment;
— specify the circumstances in which the guarantee can be *determined*;
— *exclude* all the surety's important common law rights against both the debtor and the bank.

The usual clauses

These things you must understand but you must know the purpose and effect of the *usual clauses* found in bank guarantees. Refer to your own bank's form and, if necessary, make brief notes on the following:

— the *whole debt* clause;
— the *continuing security* clause;
— the clause by which the surety's liability arises on a *written demand for repayment* being made;
— the clause making the guarantee *additional* to any security already provided by the surety;
— the *consideration* clause;
— clauses dealing with the obligation of *co-guarantors*;
— the clause stating the *period of notice* to be given by the surety before the guarantee can be determined;
— the clause by which the surety accepts the *bank's statement* of its customer's account as conclusive evidence of the amount owed by him to the bank;
— the clause excluding the Rule in *Clayton's Case (1816)*;
— the clause under which the bank is entitled to keep the guarantee uncancelled for at least six months after all the moneys secured have been repaid;
— the *ultra vires* clause;
— the *free will* clause, and any associated *attestation* clause.

Your textbook or notes may mention more or less than these but we've listed the clauses that you're most likely to be questioned upon.

Determination

Strange as it may seem, the idea of taking security is not to rely on it. Having to is often a sign of poor judgment. Lending decisions should be made on the basis of the lending proposition and not upon the strength of the security offered, although, of course, this is an important factor to consider. So, most bank guarantees are determined in accordance with the terms of the agreement, the customer repaying the money to the bank. However, a bank guarantee can be determined in the following specific situations.

1 *Notice by the guarantor* This must be in accordance with the terms of the guarantee.

2 *Notice by the bank* A banker need not first seek repayment from the principal debtor before making a demand of the surety. It is up to the latter to make sure the principal debtor makes repayment. (See what we mean about the strength of the bank's position!)

3 *Death* The principal debtor's death determines the guarantee and fixes the surety's liability. The death of the surety similarly determines the guarantee *unless*, and this is usual in bank guarantees, he has bound his personal representatives to continue it.

4 *Mental disorder* Reliable notice of the mental disorder of the principal debtor or surety determines the guarantee.

5 *Bankruptcy* Notice of an act of bankruptcy by, or the making of a receiving order against, the surety determines the guarantee.

You should have a working knowledge of the procedure to be adopted following any of the events we've listed above.

Advantages and disadvantages as security

As with all 'security' topics, you must be able to compare the advantages and disadvantages of this particular type, both in isolation and in comparison with other types. You've probably got a list or table which does this, but, if you haven't, drawing one up would be a good way to finish your study of this topic.

And finally, work through the summary diagram in Fig. 8.1.

Once you feel confident about your knowledge of this topic, try to answer the 10 multiple choice questions which follow.

125

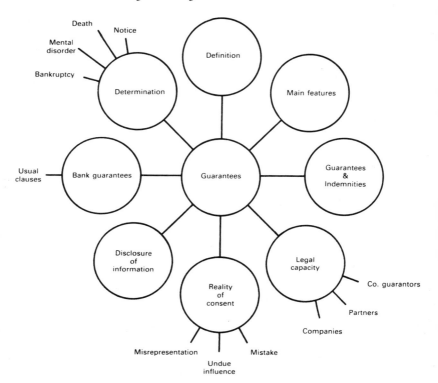

Fig. 8.1 *Guarantees*

Multiple choice questions

1 Which of the following statements concerning the nature of a guarantee is incorrect:

   a   a valid debt must exist between the creditor and the debtor?
   b   the guarantor incurs primary liability?
   c   the guarantor has no direct interest in the contract between the creditor and debtor?
   d   a guarantee must be evidenced by a written note or memorandum to be enforceable?

 answer

2 Four co-guarantors 'sign' a bank guarantee form. One of the signatures is a forgery. Under the terms of the guarantee the other three incur:

   a   no liability at all.
   b   joint liability.
   c   several liability.
   d   joint and several liability.

 answer

3 A free will clause is often included in a bank guarantee form to protect the bank against the guarantor subsequently trying to avoid the guarantee on the grounds that:

   a   he was mistaken as to the nature of what he was signing.
   b   he was misled by the bank as to the effect of the guarantee.
   c   pressure was put on him by the debtor to sign the guarantee.
   d   the bank did not disclose all the information it had about the debtor.

 answer

4 Which of the following cases is important in relation to taking a guarantee from an existing customer:

    a   *O'Hara v. Allied Irish Banks and Another* (1984)?
    b   *Lloyds Bank v. Bundy* (1975)?
    c   *National Westminster Bank plc v. Morgan* (1985)?
    d   *Saunders v. Anglia Building Society* (1970)?

5 Under a contract of guarantee, the surety is entitled to:

    a   inspect the debtor's account.
    b   know the amount of the debtor's overdraft.
    c   be informed of any material changes in the principal debtor's circumstances.
    d   make repayment at any time.

6 A contract of guarantee can be avoided if:

    a   the creditor failed to disclose all relevant facts to the surety.
    b   the surety subsequently discovers facts which, if he had known then beforehand, would have persuaded him not to give the guarantee.
    c   the creditor did not inform the surety of material changes in the debtor's circumstances.
    d   the creditor inadvertently gives an incomplete answer to a question from the surety.

7 Under a bank guarantee, the whole of the customer's indebtedness is guaranteed. This is to ensure that the guarantee:

    a   is a continuing security.
    b   avoids the rule in *Clayton's Case* (1816) working to the bank's disadvantage.
    c   prevents the surety entering a bankruptcy proof in competition with the bank.

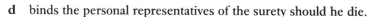

d binds the personal representatives of the surety should he die.

8 A bank guarantee entitles the bank to keep the guarantee uncancelled for at least six months after all the moneys that it secures have been repaid. This is to:

a protect the bank in case the customer's repayment is subsequently held to be a fraudulent preference.

b avoid the Rule in *Clayton's Case* (1816) working to the bank's deteriment.

c make the guarantee a continuing security.

d secure any unauthorized borrowing by the customer in this period.

9 An *ultra vires* clause will be included in a bank guarantee:

a where there is any doubt about the enforceability of the principal debt.

b where the surety is a company.

c to comply with the Companies Act 1985, s.35.

d to prevent the guarantor avoiding his obligation by a plea of undue influence.

10 Which of the following events will not determine a bank guarantee:

a death of the principal debtor?

b death of the guarantor?

c notice of an act of bankruptcy by the guarantor?

d the making of a receiving order against the guarantor?

Answers follow on pages 130-135. Score 2 marks for each correct answer.

Answers

1 The correct answer is **b**.

If you got this first question wrong, it probably means that you're uncertain about the very nature of a guarantee. The surety (guarantor) is only liable to pay if the principal debtor — the bank's customer — does not. It's under an indemnity that primary liability is incurred. 'Lend him the money he wants, if he doesn't pay you back, I will' is a guarantee. 'Lend him the money, I will see that you're repaid' is an indemnity.

A few words about the other options: a valid debt must exist between the creditor and debtor (answer **a**) — quite simply, it's impossible to guarantee something which at law doesn't exist. However, where there is any possible doubt about the validity of the originall debt, e.g. the possibility of *ultra vires* action by a company, an *ultra vires* clause will be included in the guarantee. This has the effect of making the guarantee an indemnity if the principle debt does prove to be unenforceable.

While the surety may indeed have a business interest in the contract between the creditor and debtor, e.g. where a director guarantees a loan to his company, there is no direct legal interest in that contract (answer **c**). Indeed, two quite separate and distinct contracts are involved when a guarantee is taken as security. Finally, answer **c** — the requirement that the existence of the guarantee and its terms should be provable by written evidence is laid down by the Statute of Frauds 1677.

2 The correct answer is **a**.

Co-guarantors always accept joint and several liability (answer **d**) in a bank guarantee so answers **b** and **c** can't be correct. Joint liability enables the bank to claim against any one, or any combination of the co-guarantors, usually the one(s) in the best financial position, since each is liable for the full amount. Several liability ensures that on the death or bankruptcy of a co-guarantor his estate remains liable on the guarantee.

It's a basic rule that a joint guarantee must be signed by all the co-guarantors for liability to arise on it: *National Provincial Bank v. Brackenbury* (1906), and a forged signature amounts to no signature at all: *James Graham & Co. (Timber) Ltd v. Southgate-Sands* (1985). So, answer **a** is the correct answer.

3 The correct answer is **c**.

When taking a guarantee a bank always has to be careful to check that the surety has not been pressurized into giving the security by the person whose debt he or she secures. In practice, most problems tend to arise in connection with guarantees given by wives to secure their husband's borrowing but since the Sex Discrimination Act 1975, any special treatment of a woman surety must be based on her inability to understand or appreciate the arrangement and not on the grounds of sex.

A free will clause, often accompanied by an attestation clause, is a simple way of ensuring that the surety is fully conversant with the obligations accepted under a guarantee and can't subsequently claim that the guarantee was given as a result of pressure to do so from the borrower. Remember also that the pressure could come from the bank itself: *Lloyds Bank v. Bundy* (1975) is a case in point.

A free will clause would not prevent a guarantee being set aside on the grounds of mistake (answer **a**) but a plea of *non est factum*, as it is technically known, is most unlikely to succeed (see *Saunders v. Anglia Building Society* (1970)) in any case. An attestation clause signed by the surety's independent adviser, to the effect that the nature of the document was understood, would clearly defeat such a plea.

The right to avoid the guarantee for misrepresentation (answer **b**) is one of the few important common law rights that a bank guarantee form cannot exclude, so a free will clause is of no effect here. Finally, it would not be needed for answer **d**. A contract of guarantee is not a contract to which the principle of *uberrima fides* applies and so a bank is under no duty to disclose all the information it has about the debtor; it is up to the would-be surety to enquire.

4 The correct answer is **b**.

Lloyds Bank v. Bundy (1975) is a case you should know — it's the one about the old farmer who twice mortgaged his home at the bank manager's suggestion to secure lending to his son's company. It established that a confidential relationship, very similar to a fiduciary relationship in its effect, could arise between a bank and a customer who had come to rely on the bank for advice. In the case, the bank broke the duty of care arising from this relationship by not ensuring that the old farmer received independent advice.

Let's briefly look at the other cases. In *O'Hara v. Allied Irish Banks and Another* (1984) it was held that a banker owes no duty to explain the terms and legal effects of a guarantee to a potential surety who is not a customer. *Saunders v. Anglia Building Society* (1970) is the leading case on *non est factum*, in other words the plea that the person signing a document was completely mistaken as to its nature. Since the case, it would be extremely unlikely that the plea would succeed as a defence to an action on a guarantee. Ensuring that the guarantee is signed and witnessed at the bank or attested by a solicitor would, in any case, prevent such a plea.

National Westminster Bank plc v. Morgan (1985) is an important case in contract law with direct relevance to banking. The House of Lords held that the principle of undue influence (which if proved entitles the influenced party to avoid a contract) is based on the prevention of victimization of one party by another. A presumption of undue influence will not arise merely because a confidential relationship exists between the parties; the transaction involved must be wrongful in that advantage was taken of the person subjected to the influence through the other party exercising undue influence to secure his agreement. It follows that while a banker must always be aware of his potential influence over a customer, the need for special care, e.g. insisting that the customer receives independent advice, only arises where a confidential relationship has probably arisen (as it did in *Bundy's Case*) and where the transaction proposed is clearly to the bank's advantage and the customer's disadvantage.

5 The correct answer is **d**.

The question involves the bank's duty of secrecy to his customer on the one hand and the surety's rights on the other. A surety is always entitled to know the extent of his liability under the guarantee, but this does not mean that he is invariably entitled to know the amount of the debtor's overdraft (answer **b**). Should the debit balance exceed the amount of the guarantee (it may be unauthorized or secured by some alternative security), then unless it is covered by the Consumer Credit Act 1974, the surety should be told merely that the guarantee is being fully relied on. If it is less, he can be told the actual amount of the debt. He is never, however, entitled to have or to inspect copies of the debtor's account, answer **a**. Neither, indeed, has he the right to be told of any material changes in the principal's debtor's circumstances (answer **c**), *National Westminster Bank v. Glanusk* (1913) is a case in point.

6 The correct answer is **d**.

A guarantee is not a contract *uberrimae fidei* (of the utmost good faith) as, for example, is a contract of insurance. This means that a bank is not under a duty to disclose to the would-be surety all the facts it knows which might be relevant. It's up to the surety to ask for any information that he wants. This being so, answer **a** can't be right; similarly answer **b**. You've already seen in the previous question that the creditor is not under an obligation to inform the surety of material changes in the debtor's circumstances, so answer **c** is incorrect. In practice, however, a bank would probably feel morally obliged to arrange a meeting with the debtor and surety at which the changed circumstances could be discussed. That way the bank would not be breaching its duty of secrecy while at the same time doing right by the surety. That leaves answer **d**, the correct answer. Despite the numerous exclusions in a bank guarantee, the common law still favours the surety and it was held in *Royal Bank of Scotland v. Greenshields* (1914) that any information volunteered by the creditor must be complete and true. It was also held that an entire misunderstanding of the facts by the surety must be corrected by the creditor.

7 The correct answer is **c**.

All four of the options given to you are important featues of a bank guarantee so it's well worth spending a little time considering each in turn. Establishing the guarantee as a continuing security (answer **a**) ensures that the guarantee covers any amount owing on the debtor's account at any time, subject to the usual specified limit on the surety's actual liability. It also avoids the Rule in *Clayton's Case* (1816) working to the bank's detriment. If not excluded, every payment into the account would reduce the surety's liabililty and every payment out would be a fresh advance which the guarantee would not cover. Many bank guarantees include a clause which expressly excludes the Rule — leaving nothing to chance, so to speak.

Again it is usual for the surety to bind his personal representatives should he die; again this prevents operation of the Rule in *Clayton's Case* (1816). The guarantee automatically remains in force and there is no need to break the account secured. So, to the correct answer — answer **c**. *Re Sass* (1896) established that a guarantee covering the customer's whole indebtedness prevents the surety proving against his estate in bankruptcy in competition with the bank. It also means that the surety cannot claim a part of any security held by the bank unless he meets all the customer's indebtedness.

8 The correct answer is **a**.

We've more than adequately dealt with answers **b** (*Clayton's Case*) and **c** (the guarantee as a continuing security) above, so look back if you need to. Remember, they are both important aspects of a bank guarantee; its just that neither happens to be the right answer to the question! Let's consider the other answers. It may well be that holding the guarantee uncancelled for six months would have the effect of securing unauthorized borrowing (answer **d**) but this is not the reason. It is always possible that a debtor who knows that he faced bankruptcy may try to ensure that his friends do not suffer through his misfortune. If a friend had guaranteed his overdraft it would be a natural temptation to repay the bank, if no one else, merely to protect him or her. Now, if bankruptcy proceedings should follow, the payment to the bank would arguably be a fraudulent preference in so far as the bank had been paid back before and in preference to other creditors. The bank, presumably, would be unaware of this. Since a trustee in bankruptcy is entitled to recover property which was the subject of a fraudulent preference, the bank would have to pay the sum to the trustee although it had already released the security. By the simple expedient of holding the guarantee uncancelled for a period of six months after repayment has been made, the bank protects itself against this possibility. (Look at Topic 5 for further information if you need to.)

9 The correct answer is **a**.

Ultra vires means 'beyond the power of' and is, as you know, an important principle in company law and something a banker has to be wary of; remember *Re Introductions Ltd* (1969). However, *ultra vires* clauses are aimed at remedying defects in the security caused by lack of contractual capacity in the principal debtor and not in the surety. Obvious examples include a loan to a minor and an *ultra vires* loan to a company. So, answer **b** can't be right. Answer **c** (Companies Act 1985, s.35) concerns the circumstances in which a company can be held to an *ultra vires* contract, something we cover thoroughly in Topic 4. An *ultra vires* clause is, however, something completely different. A plea of undue influence (answer **d**) when a bank has to enforce a guarantee against the surety must be avoided. This is done by a 'free will' clause, however — not by an *ultra vires* clause.

That leaves answer **a** — the correct answer — where there is any doubt about the enforceability of the principal debt. The effect of the *ultra vires* clause if the principal debt does prove unenforceable is to convert the guarantee into an indemnity. As you know, a person giving an indemnity incurs primary liability; his obligation to pay is not dependent on the non-payment by someone else. This means that the unenforceability of the principal debt is irrelevant to his own liability.

10 The correct answer is **b**.

Apologies for a bit of trick question to finish with. At common law all the events we gave you as options would determine a guarantee. However, a bank guarantee is intended to put the bank into the strongest possible position vis-à-vis the surety. Answers **a**. **b** and **d** are all situations in which the bank has the clearest interest in having the guarantee determined, but not so **b** — death of the guarantor. Hence, bank guarantees will expressly provide that the surety's personal representatives are bound by the guarantee should he die. The guarantee therefore automatically continues in force.

Score 2 marks for each correct answer. What was your score for this topic? Fill it in on the score grid.

If you scored 12 or less and are still a bit shaky on some points go back and look at the study guide again, before proceeding any further.

If you are sure you really understand and are familiar with the topic now, try the 10 further questions which are on pages 188-190.

Alternatively you can go on to the next topic and do all the post-tests together at the end.

Topic 9   Bills of Exchange

Study guide

How to approach the Topic

It's been our experience that 'Bills of Exchange' is often studied with some reluctance by students (and lecturers!) as though it somehow contained dark academic secrets which it was better not to know! Nothing could be further from the truth. It's an essentially practical subject and until such time as bits of plastic and electronic wizardry completely replace cheques (and cash?), the law and practice on bills of exchange is central to your work. Granted, you won't often handle bills other than cheques but cheques are, after all, just a particular kind of bill of exchange.

We're advising you to approach this topic in the following ways:

— Think in *money terms*, think as a *trader* would — you want to *pay* and *be paid*. Negotiable instruments in general can be said to be *documents used in commerce to secure the payment of money*. They are the creation of the commercial world.

— Study *topics* (we suggest which ones below) rather than plough through the 1882 Act section by section, as at least one leading textbook does.

You can expect *one* question (out of three) in Section C on Bills of Exchange and it will *almost certainly* be on one of the following topics:

— Whether or not a particular document is a *valid bill of exchange*.
— The *progress* of a bill through its life cycle.
— *Presentation for payment* and *dishonour* by non-payment.
— *Discharge* of a bill.
— Definitions of a *holder, holder for value* and a *holder in due course*.
— The *liabilities* of parties to a bill.
— *Payment and collection* of bills by *banks*. (A subject we cover fully in Topic 10.)

A fairly long list agreed, but if you revise each or, indeed, most of these thoroughly you should be well prepared for the question set. Remember, exam topics (if not the questions themselves) are fairly predictable; prepare for the more likely topics — it makes sense.

Quite clearly, this is a large topic so we can't give you detailed notes on everything. In any case, that would be inappropriate. The framework below is intended as a guide through your previous studies and as a prompt for your revision.

A final word (which should cheer you): the 1882 Act goes into considerable detail on procedure at times, e.g. on acceptance and dishonour of a bill of exchange. Examiners are both human and realistic; they won't be expecting you to remember or answer on the detail of such procedural matters.

What is a bill of exchange?

If possible you should learn s.3(1), or at least be able to quote it with reasonable accuracy. We stress on several occasions in this book the value of learning definitions. You can virtually apply them as a formula to many problem question, use them as a checklist and more or less inevitably arrive at the right answer. So, a bill of exchange is

> . . . an unconditional order in writing, addressed by one person to another, signed by the person giving it, requiring the person to whom it is addressed to pay on demand or at a fixed or determinable future time a sum certain in money to or to the order of a specified person or to bearer.

The definition can be broken down into the following elements. Take each in turn, look at your own notes and perhaps add a comment or two in the margin here.

— An unconditional order.
— In writing.
— Addressed by one person to another.
— Signed by the person giving it.
— To pay on demand, or at a fixed or determinable future time.
— A sum certain in money.
— To or to the order of a specified person, or to bearer.

The progress of a bill

To be a party to a bill a person must sign it. So, when a bill is first issued it is better to refer to the parties *to the transaction*: the drawer, the drawee and the payee. Of these, it is only the drawer who has actually signed. The drawer may put the bill into circulation before or after it has been *accepted* by the drawee, at which time the latter becomes the second party to it.

Acceptance   Acceptance must be written on the bill and be signed by the drawee. By accepting, the drawee (now the acceptor) promises to pay the bill when payment *becomes due* and incurs *primary liability* on it to its holder.

Be sure you know when a bill has to be *presented* for acceptance and the difference between a *general* and a *qualified* acceptance. A qualified acceptance can, of course, be treated as a *dishonour* of the bill.

Negotation   A bill is negotiated when it is transferred in such a way as to make the transferee the holder of it; a *bearer* bill by mere delivery, an *order* bill by indorsement of the holder completely by delivery.

Indorsement   By indorsing a bill, the payee or a subsequent indorsee becomes a party to the bill; in other words, he incurs liability on it.

 Try writing down the four essentials of a valid indorsement. Second, can you distinguish between 'blank', 'special' and 'restrictive' indorsements?

Presentation for payment

Sight or *time* bills must be presented on the date fixed by the bill. *Demand* bills must be presented within a reasonable time of their issue, to make the *drawer liable*, and within a reasonable time of their indorsement, to make the *indorser liable*: s.45. Delay is excused where it is caused by circumstances beyond the holder's control and not by his 'default, misconduct or negligence': s.46. (We've deliberately quoted the Act here. It's a good idea to try to use the odd phrase from it because it shows you've used it in your studies and gives a 'polish' to your answers. We think you'll agree that this short phrase is quite easy to learn and flows nicely from the pen! Be on the look out for others.)

Dishonour

A bill is dishonoured by *non-acceptance* or by *non-payment*. This is quite straightforward but some of the associated procedural rules are quite complicated. You should be aware of the rules relating to *notice* of dishonour but a question on them is unlikely. However, *noting and protest* is a good topic for a part question and is straightforward. But if you decide to learn this, then you really should learn *acceptance and payment for honour* as well.

Discharge

Most bills go through their life cycle uneventfully (the system wouldn't work otherwise) and are discharged by *payment in due course*. This is defined by s.59 as payment: (a) by or on behalf of the drawer or acceptor, (b) at or after the bill's maturity, (c) to its holder, (d) in good faith, (e) without notice that his title is defective. Study the definition; if you can remember and understand each of the aspects we've itemized, it becomes an answering formula for a question on the subject.

The other methods of discharge are: *merger, renunciation, cancellation* and *material alteration*.

Holder, holder for value and holder in due course

Holder

The starting point — defined by s.2 as 'the payee or indorsee of a bill who is in possession of it, or the bearer of a bearer bill.' Again, know and understand it. Remember, for example, that a thief of a bearer bill *is* its holder. Although he himself obtains no rights against the parties to the bill — he obviously can't sue the acceptor — a person taking the bill from him in good faith and for value (a holder in due course, in fact) can. On the other hand, remember that a person holding under a forged indorsement cannot be a holder because (by s.24) a forged signature is 'wholly inoperative'.

Holder for value

This is a holder of a bill for which consideration (value) has at some time been given, but not necessarily by the holder himself. Such a holder can enforce the bill against anyone who became a party to the bill before the value was given. The point to remember is that he obtains no better title to the bill than that possessed by the transferor.

Holder in due course

Being a holder in due course is really what negotiability is all about. It's his rights which make bills of exchange (including cheques, of course) an acceptable form of payment. His position is as strong as it can be.

Learn s.29(2) or, at least, our breakdown of it below. To be a holder in due course:

— The bill must be *complete and regular* on the face of it (this means technically correct).
— The holder must have taken it *before it was overdue.*
— The holder must have had *no notice of any previous dishonour.*
— The holder must have taken the bill *in good faith.*
— The holder must *himself* have given *value* for the bill.
— The holder must have *no notice of any defect in title* of the person who negotiated it at the time of its negotiation.

This is such an important topic it's worth us spending a little time to anticipate and answer possible questions you may have. So, a few important points for you.

1 *A holder* is presumed to be a holder in due course until fraud or illegality is admitted or proved in the acceptance, issue or negotiation of the bill. It's then up to the holder to prove that value in good faith was subsequently given for the bill.

2 A person who takes a transfer of a bearer bill from a *thief* can be a holder in due course. (A point we've made already, but it's worth repeating.)

3 The *payee* of a bill cannot be a holder in due course because the bill is issued to him, not negotiated.

4 A person who takes an order bill bearing a *forged indorsement* can't be a holder and therefore can't be a holder in due course; he is merely a wrongful possessor. This is because a forged signature is wholly inoperative (s.24) and therefore at law the bill has not been indorsed at all.

5 Finally, something which troubles many students and which is often poorly explained. Section 55(2) states that an indorser of a bill is precluded (estopoped/prevented) from denying to a holder in due course the genuineness and regularity of his signature and all previous indorsements. But we've just seen that a person taking under a forged indorsement is not a holder and therefore cannot be a holder in due course. And yet s.55(2) clearly implies that a person can be a holder in due course when a bill bears a forged indorsement, otherwise there would be no point in being precluded from denying it! In fact, in s.55(2) 'holder in due course' means a person who would have been a holder in due course but for the forgery. He has the *rights* but not the status of a holder in due course against *certain parties* to the bill. Specifically, when a question of liability arises in this situation (and you could easily be set a question involving this), persons signing the bill *after* the forgery are estopped from denying the genuiness of what is actually a forgery. The estoppel makes the bill valid and enforceable between the parties *subsquent* to the forgery. Look at Fig. 9.1.

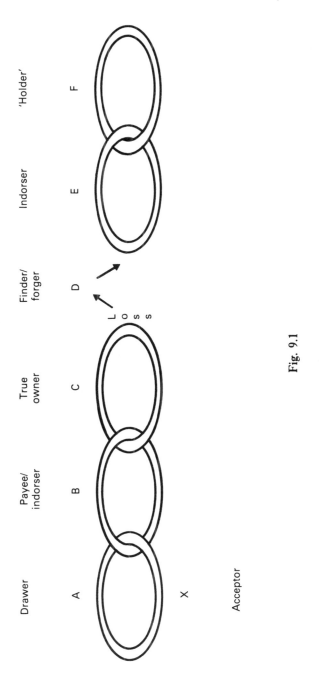

Fig. 9.1

141

Here the true owner of the bill is C but s.55(1) gives F, in fact a wrongful possessor, the rights of a holder in due course provided he would have satisfied the requirements of s.29(1) if it were not for the break in the chain of negotiation. While D's finding of the bill and forgery of C's signature breaks the chain of negotiation and title, thereby preventing F from enforcing the bill against A, B or C, he can enforce the bill against E because s.55(2) precludes E from denying that D's forgery of C's indorsement is in fact genuine. C, still the true owner of the bill, can bring an action in conversion against E or F for the value of the bill or its return and E is most likely to stand the loss. If C can recover the bill he can still enforce it against X, the acceptor.

And finally(!), the rights of a holder in due course: be sure you fully understand what is meant by *taking free from equities* and being able to *tranfer his title* as holder in due course to any person for value or as a gift, provided that that person was not a party to any defect which affected the bill.

Liability of parties

A party to a bill of exchange is a person who has *signed* it: i.e. the drawer, acceptor and any indorser.

The drawer (s.55)

— *Promises* that the bill will be duly accepted and paid when presented and that he will compensate any holder or indorser who has had to pay if the bill is dishonoured, provided that the proper procedure for dishonour is followed.

— *Cannot deny* to a holder in due course the payee's existence or his capacity to indorse the bill.

The acceptor (s.54)

— *Promises* that he will pay the bill in accordance with his acceptance.

— *Cannot deny* to a holder in due course the drawer's existence, the genuineness of his signature and his power to draw the bill.

— *Cannot deny* the drawer's capacity to indorse the bill if it is payable to his order.

— *Cannot deny* the existence, or the capacity to indorse, of a third person (the payee) to whom the bill is made payable.

Section 54(1) means that the acceptor cannot refuse payment to a holder in due course by proving that the drawer does not exist or that his signature was forged or that he had no capacity or authority to draw the bill, for example, where a clerk draws a bill for employer and signs on his employer's behalf. This is, in fact, an application of estoppel very similar to that under s.55 which we discussed above. If the drawer's signature was forged, the bill is not really a bill at all (think about s.3(1)) and therefore there can't be a holder, let alone a holder in due course. So, the possessor, the apparent holder in due course, has the *rights* of a holder in due course against the acceptor although, in reality, he is not even a holder.

The acceptor does not warrant, however, that an indorsement is either genuine or valid. This means that he can set up a forged indorsement against a person seeking to enforce the bill against him. The forged signature, as we've stressed already, is entirely without effect and breaks the chain of title from the acceptor to the possessor.

An indorser (s.55)

— *Promises* that the bill will be *duly accepted and paid* when presented.

— *Promises to compensate* any party who has had to pay as a result of its dishonour, provided that the proper procedure for dishonour is followed.

— *Cannot deny* to a holder in due course the genuiness and regularity of the drawer's signature, or of any indorsements prior to his own.

— *Cannot deny* to a subsequent indorsee that it was a valid bill when he indorsed it, nor that his title to it was good.

So, an indorser is responsible to all persons who became parties to the bill after he did. He is also responsible to the holder. If the drawer's signature proves to be a forgery, the possessor of the 'bill' (remember that it won't actually be a bill) has the *rights* of a holder in due course against all indorsers, as well as against the acceptor and, if an indorsement is forged, the same rights against any person who indorsed the bill subsequent to the forgery.

Right, on to the summary diagram (Fig. 9.2).

Once you feel confident about your knowledge of this topic, try to answer the 10 multiple choice questions which follow.

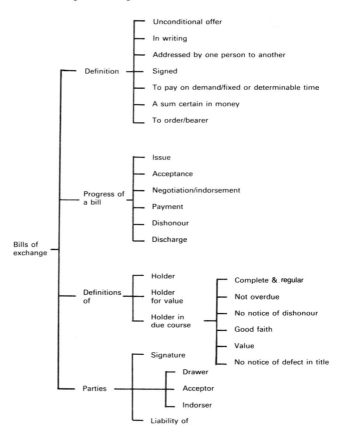

Fig. 9.2 *Bills of exchange*

Multiple choice questions

1   Which of the following legal characteristics of a bill of exchange is not stated with complete accuracy:

   a   title is transferable by delivery?
   b   a person taking a transfer in good faith and for value is not affected by any defects in the title of the transferor?
   c   the holder can sue in his own name?
   d   the holder need not give notice to prior parties to establish his title?

2   When a bill of exchange is issued, how many parties are there to the transaction:

   a   1?
   b   2?
   c   3?
   d   4?

3   Which of the following would be invalid wording on a bill of exchange:

   a   pay A or order £5,000 on or before 30 June 1986?
   b   pay B or order £5,000 on 30 June 1986 with interest at 10% per annum?
   c   pay C or order £5,000 in three equal instalments due 30 April 1986, 31 May 1986 and 30 June 1986?
   d   pay D or order £5,000 on 30 June 1986 and charge the same to the proceeds of sale of 1,000 tons of wheat shipped per *SS. Angelides*?

4   A draws a cheque in favour of B for goods supplied to him; B negotiates the cheque to C as a gift. In this situation, which of the following statements is incorrect:

a   B can enforce the cheque against A?
b   C can enforce the cheque against A?
c   C can enforce the cheque against B?
d   both B and C can enforce the cheque against A?

 *answer*

5   In which of the following cases did estoppel not operate:

a   *Bank of England v. Vagliano Brothers* (1891)?
b   *Greenwood v. Martins Bank* (1933)?
c   *Wealden Woodlands (Kent) Ltd v. National Westminster Bank Ltd* (1983)?
d   *London Joint Stock Bank Ltd v. Macmillan and Arthur* (1918)?

 *answer*

6   Which of the following is a holder within the meaning of s.2:

a   a person who has stolen a bearer bill?
b   a person who has stolen an order bill?
c   a person who has found an order bill?
d   a person holding under a forged indorsement?

 *answer*

7   Which of the following sections of the 1882 Act deals with forged and unauthorized signatures:

a   s.2?
b   s.20?
c   s.24?
d   s.29?

 *answer*

8 A draws a bill on B, who accepts, payable to C or to bearer. The bill is stolen by D who negotiates it for value and in good faith to E. E gives it to F as a present. On the facts as given F can enforce the bill against:

    a A, B, C, D, or E.
    b A, B, C or D.
    c D or E.
    d E.

9 Noting and protest applies only:

    a to foreign bills.
    b where an acceptance or payment for honour is sought.
    c where a bill is dishonoured by an acceptor for honour.
    d where a bill of exchange is dishonoured.

10 A referee in case of need is a person who:

    a will provide a financial status reference for the holder of a bill should a prospective transferee require it.
    b arbitrates in the High Court in cases involving bills of exchange.
    c undertakes to pay a bill of exchange after it has been protested for dishonour.
    d is designated on the bill by the drawer as a person to whom the holder may apply for payment if the drawee dishonours the bill.

Answers follow on pages 148-151. Score 2 marks for each correct answer.

Answers

1 The correct answer is **a**.

You should have got this one right. Bearer bills are transferred by delivery alone but an order bill is transferred by indorsement completed by delivery. Option **a** only made mention of transfer by delivery.
A few words about the other options. 'In good faith' means without knowing or suspecting that all is not as it should be concerning the bill; 'for value' means for consideration — in return for something of value. Suing in his own name and not having to give notice to prior parties to establish his title are both ways in which negotiability differs from assignment, from which the former developed.

2 The correct answer is **c**.

A party to a bill of exchange is a person who has signed the bill and thereby incurred liability upon it. When a bill is first issued, only the drawer signs it and therefore is the only party to it. However, every bill will identify a drawee (the person on whom the bill is drawn) and a payee (the person to whom payment is to be made). This being the case, it's more useful to refer to the parties to the transaction, for then both the drawee and the payee are included. The question asked for parties to the transaction. Remember that when the drawee becomes the acceptor by signing the bill he becomes a party. So does the payee if, instead of holding on to the bill until its maturity, he negotiates it, indorsing it in the process.

3 The correct answer is **a**.

It's the words 'on or before' which would invalidate the bill in answer **a**. They don't satisfy the 1882 Act's requirement that payment be stated to be 'at a fixed or determinable future date'. Payment with interest (answer **b**) and payment in instalments (answer **c**) are still payments of a 'sum certain in money' by s.9(1). The direction in answer **d** to charge the bill to the proceeds of a specified sale does not affect the order to pay to the drawee. The bill is still an 'unconditional order' within s.3(1) since s.3(3) specifically provides that the drawer may indicate a particular fund out of which the drawee is to reimburse himself.

4 The correct answer is **c**.

This question involves consideration. While a bill is enforceable providing consideration has at some time been given for it, as between immediate parties, i.e. transferor and transferee, consideration is necessary to enforce the bill. Since B gave the bill to C as a gift, C has given no consideration for the bill and therefore cannot enforce it against him. All the other three answers are accurate statements.

5 The correct answer is **c**.

First of all, are you sure what is meant by 'estoppel'? Well, estoppel is a rule of evidence which prevents a person from denying the truth of a statement he has made to a person who has relied on it and altered his position as a consequence. It's of considerable importance in this Topic. So, let's look at the nature of the estoppel in each of the answers.

In *Bank of England v. Vagliano Brothers* (1891), a very well known case involving a 'fictitious payee', the defendant informed the Bank of England that the bills which were the subject of the case would be presented for payment in due course. This was held to amount to an affirmation that the signatures on the bills (those of a fraudulent employee) were genuine and they could not subsequently deny this.

In *Greenwood v. Martins Bank* (1933), perhaps the classic case of estoppel involving a bill of exchange, the plaintiff, some eight months after first discovering that his wife had been forging his signature on cheques, informed the bank and sought repayment of the amount of the forged cheques. Clearly, his silence when he had known what was going on for so long amounted to an affirmation that the signatures were genuine and the bank was entitled to debit his account with the amount of the cheques.

In *Wealden Woodlands (Kent) Ltd v. National Westminster Bank Ltd* (1983), however, a case also involving forgery of the drawer's signature, a plea of estoppel by the bank failed because, on the facts, the company had not been to blame in any way for its failure to notice and query the forgeries and could not be said to have adopted them.

Lastly, in *London Joint Stock Bank Ltd v. Macmillan and Arthur* (1918), a very important case specifically concerning cheques, the defendants' negligence in signing a cheque drawn in a way which made fraudulent alterations easy prevented them from denying the genuiness of the altered cheque. The case is, of course, authority for the basic rule that a customer owes his bank a duty to draw cheques with reasonable care.

6 The correct answer is **a**.

This is the sort of question and options which often catch students out. So, think about it. Section 2 states that a holder is 'the payee or indorsee of a bill who is in possession of it, or the bearer of a bearer bill'. Hence, answer **a** has got to be right. What about the others? A person who steals (answer **b**) or finds (answer **c**) an order bill is certainly neither the payee nor the indorsee. Thus, neither can be a holder. Since a forged signature is 'wholly inoperative' (s.24) a person holding under a forged indorsement can't be the indorsee and therefore can't be the holder of the bill.

One final point to conclude: the person in possession of the bill in answers **b**, **c** and **d** can't transfer title since he has none to transfer, but not so the person in answer **a**. Since title to a bearer bill transfers by delivery alone, a person taking a transfer in good faith and for value etc. can gain a perfectly valid title to the bill. He is, of course, a holder in due course. Remember too the special meaning of 'holder in due course' for the purposes of s.55.

7   The correct answer is **c**.

Some of the sections that you should try to remember. Section 24 provides that a forged or unauthorized signature is wholly inoperative. In fact it is no signature at all. To the rule there are two exceptions. First s.60, which protects a banker who pays a cheque bearing a forged indorsement (we look at this in Topic 10), and second, estoppel, which we looked at above.

Now for the other sections. Section 2 (answer **a**) is a general definition and interpretation clause defining, among other terms, 'holder' and containing the rather unhelpful definition of a banker as someone who 'carries on the business of banking'. Section 20 (answer **b**) deals with inchoate (incompletely drawn) instruments, a blank cheque for example. The person to whom an inchoate instrument is issued has *prima facie* authority to complete the bill for any amount. Section 29 (answer **d**) is perhaps the most important single section in the Act; it defines a holder in due course. You should make an attempt to learn s.29(1).

8   The correct answer is **b**.

Did you spot that the bill in question was a bearer bill? If you didn't, you almost certainly got the question wrong, probably choosing answer **c** although this would have been incorrect here as well! Let's think about the situation. The bill is a bearer bill and therefore title to it transfers by delivery. Although D stole the bill he was still the holder of it and while he himself could not enforce the bill against prior parties, he can transfer title to a holder in due course, E in this case. (It's the drawback of issuing a bearer bill.) If E is a holder in due course, we can presume that F is as well. As such he can enforce it against all prior parties except E. Since he took the bill as a gift, he gave no consideration for it. This being the case, a short cut to the correct answer would have been to say that any answer with party E in it couldn't be right. That left just the correct answer, answer **b**.

9   The correct answer is **d**.

Noting is the formal representation of a dishonoured bill by a notary public for acceptance or payment. The reply given is noted on the bill. The protest takes the form of a formal declaration signed by the notary attesting the dishonour and containing the relevant facts. Where a notary isn't available, a householder in the presence of two witnesses may give a certificate equivalent to the protest.

Now to the question: it was a bit of trick question in reality. While the Act specifies that a dishonoured bill must be noted and protested in the situations in answers **a**, **b** and **c**, the procedure can be adopted when any bill is dishonoured, so **d** is the right answer. The advantage of noting and protesting a dishonoured bill is that it provides formal evidence of dishonour which will be universally recognized and accepted.

10   The correct answer is **d**.

Answers **a** and **b** are both plausible but neither is right. Answer **c** refers to an acceptor for honour: a person who is not already a party to the bill and who accepts the bill for part or all of the amount after it has been either protested for dishonour by non-acceptance or protested for better security. The holder of the bill must consent to the acceptance for honour since it prevents him exercising his right of recourse against other parties to the bill. That leaves answer **d**. Note that a referee in case of need is designated on the bill by the drawer when he issues it, that it must be protested for non-payment before payment is sought from the referee, and that the holder is not obliged to look to him for payment.

Score 2 marks for each correct answer. What was your score for this topic? Fill it in on the score grid.

If you scored 12 or less and are still a bit shaky on some points go back and look at the study guide again, before proceeding any further.

If you are sure you really understand and are familiar with the topic now, try the 10 further questions which are on pages 190-192.

Alternatively you can go on to the next topic and do all the post-tests together at the end.

Topic 10   Cheques

Study guide

In our introductory section 'How to Use this Book' we said that one of the objectives of the Short Answer Tests was to enable you to determine an order for your revision. We're going to vary the plan a little now. Since 'Cheques' logically follows on from Topic 9: Bills of Exchange we're suggesting that you should study Topic 9 *before* you study this Topic. This doesn't of course invalidate your revision campaign — it merely alters the actual implementation of it.

On a sort of revision cost–benefit analysis, this Topic scores high. There will almost certainly be two questions out of three set on 'Cheques' in Part C of the examination paper. Don't think, however, that these two questions will invariably involve just cheques; they could involve the general law on bills of exchange or require comparisons to be made with other types of bills of exchange. So, how should you tackle the Topic?

The general legal framework

You'll see from the structure of this Study Guide that we're dividing the Topic into *three main parts*, the first being the general legal framework. Here you need to study the following things:

— The *definition* of a cheque.
— The points of *comparison* between cheques and other bills of exchange. One word of a short phrase should be enough to act as a memory jog, so make a note of them. We're giving you the first one: Acceptance. . . .
— *Crossed cheques* Make sure you can answer the following questions. What is a crossing? What are the different types of crossings and what are their different effects? (Don't forget cheques which are crossed 'Account Payee', although the words are not part of the crossing at all.) Who may cross a cheque? Make sure that you have concise notes covering all these points and can deal with them without hesitation.

The general legal framework is straightforward although it does of course include the applicable sections of the Bills of Exchange Act 1882. Of greater importance to you, both in your day-to-day work and for the exam, are the position of a 'Paying Banker' and of a 'Collecting Banker'.

The paying banker

You're almost certain to be asked a question involving paying bankers so we're going to go into rather more detail than we did on the general legal framework.

The paying banker's duty

A banker owes a *contractual duty* to pay a customer's cheques provided (a) they are properly drawn; (b) sufficient funds are available or an agreed overdraft facility exists; (c) there is no legal bar to payment; and (d) the customer has not revoked his authority to pay.

Termination of authority to pay

Learn the following:
  (a) *Countermand* of payment.
  (b) *Legal bars*: garnishee orders and injunctions.
  (c) Notice of the customer's *death*.
  (d) Notice of the customer's *mental disorder*.
  (e) Notice of a *bankruptcy petition* against the customer.
  (f) The making of a *winding-up order* or a *receiving order* against the customer.
  (g) Where the cheque is a *misapplication of funds*.
  (h) Knowledge of a *defect in the presenter's title*.
Take each of these specific instances in turn and make sure you understand them. Add a brief note to them if you wish. Different books and different teachers will present these instances in slightly different ways. Don't worry, each will be right, we're sure; the important thing is that *you* understand them.

A paying banker's liability

This takes three forms: wrongfully debiting an account, wrongfully dishonouring a cheque and paying someone other than the true owner.
  Wrongfully debiting an account occurs where:

153

— The customer has *countermanded* (stopped) payment of a cheque.
— Possibly, where the bank pays a *post-dated cheque* before the proper date for payment.
— Where the customer's signature has been *forged*, but don't forget the possibility of the customer being *estopped* from denying the genuiness of the signature as in *Greenwood Martins Bank Ltd* (1932).
— Where the cheque has been *materially altered* without the customer's consent — usually a fraudulent increase in the amount of the cheque. Remember the Rule in *London Joint Stock Bank v. Macmillan and Arthur* (1918) here.

Wrongfully dishonouring a cheque gives rise to liability for *breach of contract* and, possibly, for *libel*.

Liability for conversion The tort of conversion is committed where a person deals with property belonging to another in a manner which denies the owner's title and right to possess the property. A banker commits conversion if he pays a cheque to anyone other than its true owner. Clearly, a banker needs protection against innocently committing the tort since he is rarely in a position to know whether the presenter of the cheque is its true owner. So, this is what we look at next.

The paying banker's protection

The first point to make is that unless the customer is estopped from denying its genuiness, a bank has *no protection* if it pays a cheque on which its customer's signature is *forged*. Nevertheless, statute affords considerable protection and you *must* know the relevant sections; a question on them is very likely.

— *Forged and unauthorized indorsements* The Bills of Exchange Act 1882, s.60 protects a banker against liability to the holder (the true owner) if he pays a cheque which bears a forged or unauthorized indorsement provided he pays in good faith and in the ordinary course of business.
    Although the Cheques Act 1957, s.1 has greatly reduced the importance of this section (see below), it remains important wherever indorsement of a cheque is still necessary. Remember, s.60 applies *only* to cheques and not to bills of exchange generally.
— *Crossed cheques* The Bills of Exchange Act 1882, s.79(2) protects the payment of a cheque in good faith and without negligence on which the crossing is not apparent, or on which the crossing has been obliterated, added to or altered and this is

not apparent. *Section 80* protects a banker against liability to a cheque's true owner if he pays in good faith, without negligence and in accordance with the crossing. In practice, these two sections are far less important than s.60 because by far the most likely defect on a cheque is a forged or unauthorized indorsement.

— *Unindorsed or irregularly indorsed cheques* By the Cheques Act 1957, s.1, a banker who pays a cheque drawn on him which is not indorsed or which is irregularly indorsed is considered to have paid it in due course provided he pays it in good faith and in the ordinary course of business.

Finally, although it's fairly unlikely, you could get a question which involves the payment of *conditional orders*, *bankers' drafts* or *dividend or interest* warrants. What protection has a paying banker in these cases? Also, what is the position when a cheque card is used? This is important in practice because a cheque is frequently not acceptable as payment unless it is backed by a cheque card.

The collecting banker

As with the 'paying banker', you're almost certain to be set a question which involves a collecting banker in some way or other.

The collecting banker's duty

A banker owes a contractual duty to his customer to collect cheques and other payment instruments on his behalf. In so doing, he owes a duty of care to his customer. For example, he must follow normal collection procedures in presenting a cheque for payment.

The collecting banker's liability

It follows from what we've just said above that a collecting banker will incur liability for *breach of contract* to his customer if he fails to exercise reasonable care in the collection of his customer's cheques and other instruments. In addition, he commits the tort of *conversion* against its true owner if he collects a cheque on behalf of a customer who is not entitled to it. Since conversion can be committed innocently and since bankers collect vast numbers of cheques every working day, they must receive reasonable protection at law if they are to fulfil their role.

The collecting banker's statutory protection

This is provided by the Cheques Act 1957, s.4. The wording of the section may seem a little more complicated than its effect.

The section *applies* where a banker in *good faith* and *without negligence*:

(a) receives payment *for a customer* of an instrument to which the section applies; or

(b) having credited a customer's account with the amount of such an instrument, receives payment thereof *for himself*.

It *provides* that a banker incurs no liability to the true owner of the instrument where his customer has either a defective title or no title at all to the instrument merely because he received payment of it.

The following instruments are covered by s.4: *cheques, conditional orders,* 'cheques' made payable to *impersonal payees, dividend* and *interest warrants, Paymaster General Warrants* and *bankers' drafts*.

What you must remember is that to be protected by s.4, a banker must act:

— for a customer,
— in good faith,
— without negligence.

However, knowing the conditions for s.4's application as theoretical propositions is not what you're going to be examined on; you'll be asked to apply s.4 to practical situations, usually involving a question of possible negligence. Although each case of alleged negligence must almost by definition be judged in the end on its own facts, there are accepted guides to what is likely to be negligence on a bank's part in the collection of cheques. Below, we're given you a list of such situations and the name of a leading case for each. Try your best to learn these — it's likely to be time well spent.

Instances of negligence

— Failure to make *reasonable enquiries* before opening an account: *Ladbroke & Co v. Todd* (1914); *Marfani & Co Ltd v. Midland Bank Ltd* (1968).

— Failure to *check information* disclosed under the Business Names Act 1985: *Smith and Baldwin v. Barclays Bank Ltd* (1944).

— Failure to obtain the name of its *customer's employer* or, in the case of married customers, the name of the spouse's employer: *Lloyds Bank Ltd v. E B Savory & Co* (1933).

— Crediting cheques payable to a company to the *private account* of an *official* of the company: *A L Underwood v. Bank of Liverpool and Martins Ltd* (1924).

— Crediting a *private account* of an *agent* or of an *employee* with cheques drawn by him on the account of his principal or employer: *Midland Bank Ltd v. Reckitt* (1933).

— Crediting an *agent's private account* with cheques payable to him in his capacity as an agent: *Marquess of Bute v. Barclays Bank Ltd* (1955).

— Crediting cheques payable to the *holder of a public office* to his private account: *Ross v. London City Westminster and Parr's Bank Ltd* (1919).

— Collecting *without satisfactory explanation* a cheque payable to a limited company for the account of another company: *London & Montrose Shipbuilding & Repairing Co v. Barclays Bank Ltd* (1926).

— Collecting *without satisfactory explanation* cheques for amounts inconsistent with its customer's activities: *Nu-Stilo Footwear Ltd v. Lloyds Bank Ltd* (1956).

— Collecting *without satisfactory explanation* third party cheques where the customer has previously proved to be unreliable: *Motor Traders Guarantee Corporation Ltd v. Midland Bank Ltd* (1937).

— Collecting third party cheques *without sufficient enquiry* where the circumstance demand it: *Baker v. Barclays Bank Ltd* (1955).

— Collecting *without sufficient explanation* 'Account payee' cheques for someone other than the named payee'. *House Property Co. of London Ltd & Others v. London County & Westminster Bank Ltd* (1915).

Finally, remember that when a banker is unable to rely on s.4, he can plead the Law Reform (Contributory Negligence) Act 1945. A successful plea will reduce the damages awarded.

Protection as holder in due course

Section 4 protects a banker when he acts as agent *for his customer*. If, however, he gives *value* for the cheque he will be collecting *for himself* as holder for value. Although s.4 no longer applies, if he can establish himself as holder in due course he has an alternative and perfect defence to an action for conversion of the cheque: at law he is its *true owner*. It makes no difference that he may have acted negligently (compare s.4) although taking an order cheque bearing a forged indorsement prevents him from becoming a holder (again, compare s.4). Make sure you know what constitutes giving value on the part of a bank.

Now work through the summary diagram in Fig. 10.1.

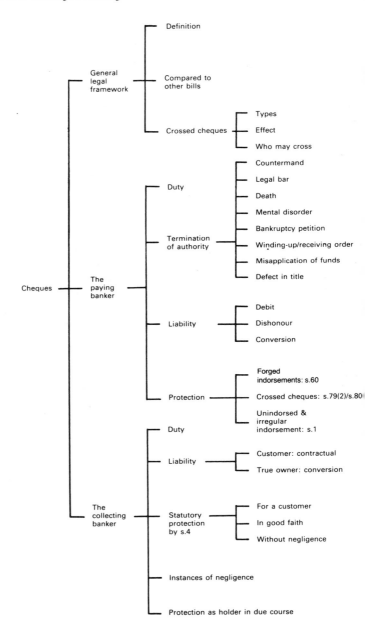

Fig. 10.1 *Cheques*

Once you feel confident about your knowledge of this Topic, try to answer the 10 multiple choice questions which follow.

Multiple choice questions

1 A cheque differs from other bills of exchange in that:

    a it can be made out to 'cash'.
    b it is the only instrument that can be crossed.
    c it cannot be negotiated by indorsement.
    d it is never accepted.

 _answer_

2 Which of the following does not form part of a crossing on a cheque:

    a two transverse parallel lines?
    b the name of a particular bank?
    c the words 'Not negotiable'?
    d the words 'Account payee'?

 _answer_

3 Which of the following circumstances does not terminate a bank's authority to pay its customer's cheques:

    a a written countermand of payment?
    b notice of its customer's death?
    c A bankruptcy petition against its customer?
    d the making of a winding-up order against its customer?

 _answer_

4 A bank is invariably liable to its customer if it pays a cheque:

    a which has been materially altered by a third party.
    b on which the customer's signature was forged.
    c after payment has been countermanded.
    d before the proper date for payment.

 _answer_

5 Which of the following prevents a banker relying on the Bills of Exchange Act 1882, s.60:

    a payment after normal banking hours?

    b negligence?

    c the lack of an indorsement where one is necessary?

    d the fact that the cheque was uncrossed?

 *answer*

6 X pays into his account four cheques:

    i A bearer cheque which he had taken in good faith but which the transferor had found.

    ii A cheque made out to Y & Co and indorsed with his own signature by Y to X.

    iii A cheque made out to Y & Co on which the indorsement of Y & Co had been forged.

    iv A cheque made payable to him which he had found in a desk drawer after six months.

Payment of which of these cheques would be specifically protected by the Cheques Act 1957, s.1:

    a i?

    b ii?

    c iii?

    d iv?

 *answer*

7 The Cheques Act 1957, s.4(2) can apply:

    a only to cheques.

    b only to crossed cheques.

    c only to cheques and other bills of exchange.

    d to documents which are not bills of exchange.

 *answer*

8 *Marfani & Co. Ltd v. Midland Bank Ltd* (1968):

    a established that a collecting banker cannot rely on the Rule in *London Joint Stock Bank v. Macmillan and Arthur* (1918).

    b indicates that contemporary banking practice is a better guide than previous decisions to what constitutes negligence when collecting a cheque.

c established that failure to obtain the name of the employer of a married woman customer's husband is *prima facie* evidence of negligence.

b established that opening an account before all references have been received prevents a collecting banker relying on the Cheques Act 1957, s.4.

9 A banker must make enquiries before collecting a cheque for someone other than the named payee:

a crossed 'Not negotiable'.
b crossed 'Account payee'.
c neither of the above.
d both of the above.

10 Which of the following circumstances prevents a collecting bank being the holder in due course of a cheque it collects:

a negligence on its part when collecting the cheque?
b lack of an indorsement?
c a forged indorsement?
d payment of the cheque into an overdrawn account in the ordinary course of business?

Answers follow on pages 163-167. Score 2 marks for each correct answer.

Answers

1 The correct answer is **d**.

A banker never accepts a cheque drawn on him (answer **d**); for a start it would be completely impractical! This means, of course, that the holder can't sue the bank if the cheque is unpaid; his only course of action is against the drawer of the cheque and any subsequent indorser.

Although 'cheques' are often made out to cash, they are not cheques at all because no payee is specified. So, answer **a** can't be correct. Remember, however, that a 'cheque' made out to 'cash' or to 'wages' is a valid order from the customer to the banker to pay the stated amount from the account.

Answer **b** is wrong because although other bills can't be crossed, other instruments can, e.g. postal and money orders. Lastly, answer **c** is wrong because cheques can be negotiated in exactly the same way as other bills. Of course, a negotiated cheque is fairly rare.

2 The correct answer is **d**.

A crossing is a direction to the paying banker. The words 'Account Payee' (answer **d**) are not part of a crossing because they are a direction to the collecting banker, not the paying banker. Nevertheless, to ignore them constitutes *prima facie* evidence of negligence.

Two transverse parallel lines (answer **a**) are a general crossing; the name of a particular bank (answer **b**) is a special crossing, to which two transverse parallel lines may be added. The words 'Not negotiable' (answer **c**) may be added to either a general or a special crossing. Remember, contrary to what you might suppose, the words 'Not negotiable' do not affect a cheque's transferability only its negotiability.

3 The correct answer is **c**.

Until notice of the bankruptcy petition is received, the Bankruptcy Act 1914, s.46 protects payments to the debtor or to his assignee. It does not, however, protect payments to third parties although there is debate on this point. (See generally Topic 5.)

A written countermand (answer **a**) terminates a banker's authority to pay a cheque but remember that it must come to the banker's actual attention: *Curtice v. London City and Midland Bank Ltd* (1908). Again, remember that it's notice of a customer's death, not the death itself, which terminates the authority (answer **b**): Bills of Exchange Act 1882, s.75. The making of a winding-up order (answer **d**) terminates the authority to pay cheques, whether or not the bank has notice of it.

4 The correct answer is **c**.

Answer **c** is correct provided, of course, that the countermand was in writing, technically correct and had come to the actual attention of the bank. Other methods of 'stopping' a cheque may justify postponing payment until enquiries have been made but they don't actually constitute a valid countermand.

Where a bank pays a cheque which has been materially altered by a third party (answer **a**) it would most likely be liable but the Rule in *London Joint Stock Bank v. Macmillan and Arthur* (1918) imposes a duty on customers to draw cheques with reasonable care to avoid them being fraudulently altered. So, answer **a** is not absolutely correct.

In 99.9% of cases answer **b** — where the customer's signature has been forged on the cheque — would be correct but a customer can be estopped (prevented or precluded) from denying the genuiness of a forged signature. *Greenwood v. Martins Bank Ltd* (1932) is one such case. Here the plaintiff waited some eight months before informing the bank that his wife (by then dead) had been forging his signature on cheques.

Where a bank pays a cheque before the proper date for payment (answer **d**) the bank would have paid without authority. However, questions of liability only arise when other cheques are dishonoured for apparent lack of funds through the cheque being paid early, perhaps before a countermand of the postdated cheque.

5 The correct answer is **c**.

The Bills of Exchange Act 1882, s.60 protects a banker against liability to the true owner of a cheque if he pays a cheque bearing a forged or unauthorized indorsement provided he pays in good faith and in the ordinary course of business. Paying a cheque without an indorsement where one is required (answer **c**) would never be payment 'in the ordinary course of business'. You might think that payment after normal banking hours (answer **a**) would prevent s.60 applying for the same reason, but what of a customer being attended to at closing time? In *Baines v. National Provincial Bank Ltd* (1927), it was held that a bank is allowed a reasonable time to complete its business after its advertised closing time. In that particular case the bank was allowed to debit its customer's account with a cheque cashed five minutes after closing time and a countermand the following morning was ineffective.

'Good faith' in s.60 means 'honesty' and a negligent payment (answer **b**) is still a payment in good faith: *Carpenters' Co. v. British Mutual Banking Co.* (1938). Finally, s.60 applies to both crossed and uncrossed cheques, so answer **d** can't be correct. Remember, however, that payment of a crossed cheque over the counter would not be 'in the ordinary course of business' and the protection of s.60 would be lost.

6 The correct answer is **b**.

Let's begin by reminding ourselves of what s.1 actually says. Under the section, a banker who pays a cheque drawn on him which is not indorsed or which is irregularly indorsed is considered to have paid it in due course provided he pays it (i) in good faith, and (ii) in the ordinary course of business. Answer **b** is the only option which comes within the protection given. Y should have indorsed the cheque in the name of Y & Co since the cheque was made out to Y & Co. His indorsement, while genuine enough, was irregular because it wasn't in the same name as the payee of the cheque. On the facts given the payment was in good faith and in the ordinary course of business, so s.1 would operate.

Since title to a bearer cheque (answer **a**) passes by mere delivery, it is unnecessary to indorse it; indeed any indorsement that it bears can be ignored. So, in this case the protection of s.1 would not be necessary in any case.

Answer **c** involved a forged indorsement, not an irregular one. So, s.1 can't be applicable. You should have remembered that the Bills of Exchange Act 1882, s.60 is the appropriate section here. This protects a banker against liability to the holder if he pays a cheque which bears a forged or unauthorized indorsement provided he pays in good faith and in the ordinary course of business. Although the question didn't ask this, on the facts there is nothing to suggest that s.60 would not have protected the payment.

Finally, answer **d**: this situation is potentially within the protection of s.1 but the cheque is 'stale' and its payment would probably not be in the ordinary course of business. So, **d** can't be the right answer.

7 The correct answer is **d**.

Rather a tricky question this; most, if not all, of the examples of s.4 operating that you will have covered will have involved cheques. However, the section also applies to (i) conditional orders, (ii) 'cheques' made payable to cash or to wages, (iii) dividend and interest warrants, (iv) Paymaster General Warrants and (v) bankers' drafts. Immediately, you can see that answers **a** and **b** can't be right. Answer **c** gives a wider range of application than **a** or **b** but s.4 does not apply to bills of exchange other than cheques. However, it does apply, as you've seen above, to a number of instruments which are not bills of exchange, e.g. conditional orders and 'cheques' made out to cash. To summarize then, the section applies to a number of different instruments, both crossed and uncrossed, but it does not apply to bills of exchange other than cheques.

8 The correct answer is **b**.

It's not the end of the world if you can't remember the names of all the cases you will have been given in your notes. However, you should try to remember the names of the really important ones such as *Marfani's Case*. The decision is considered to mark a break with the previous practice of relying on a stricter application of precedent in cases of potential negligence in the collection of cheques. To come extent, each case can be decided on its own facts although there are, of course, well established guidelines. Remember, however, that it's quite possible for the courts to hold modern banking practice to be negligent whatever you, your manager or head office may think.

Now for the other answers: the Rule in *London Joint Stock Bank v. Macmillan and Arthur* (1918) (answer **a**) does not apply to collecting bankers, that much is perfectly correct, but this was established by the decision itself and had nothing to do with *Marfani's Case*. It's very important to obtain details of a customer's employer (answer **c**) but this was decided in *Lloyds Bank Ltd v. E B Savory & Co* (1933). What's your bank's practice on obtaining details of who employs a married woman customer's husband? How does this square with the Sex Discrimination Act 1975? Finally, answer **d**: obtaining, and checking, references is normally an essential stage in the process of opening an account unless the applicant is already known to the bank. However, *Marfani's Case* itself shows that it's impossible to be categoric about this. If you remember, the account was opened even though one referee never replied, yet the bank was still able to rely on the protection of s.4.

9 The correct answer is **b**.

Don't forget that the words 'Account Payee' (answer **b**) are not actually part of the crossing. A crossing is an instruction to the paying bank, the words are an instruction to the collecting bank. Remember also that a banker is only under an obligation to make reasonable enquiries in order to retain the protection of s.4. In *Crumplin v. London Joint Stock Bank* (1913) it was held that there is no duty on a bank to make enquiries before collecting a cheque crossed 'Not negotiable' (answer **a**). The effect of these words is to take away a cheque's negotiability — the cheque is always transferred subject to any existing defects in title — but they don't affect its transferability. We don't need to comment on answers **c** and **d**.

10 The correct answer is **d**.

This is a difficult question. To become a holder in due course of a cheque, a bank must satisfy the Bills of Exchange Act 1882, s.29(1).

Among other things, it requires the person taking the transfer to have acted in good faith. We've already seen in these answers that 'good faith' means honesty and that acting negligently is not acting in bad faith. This being so, negligence when collecting the cheque (answer a) can't be the right answer. Negligence, remember, prevents a bank relying on the protection of s.4 of the Cheques Act 1957. Answer **b** is wrong because s.2 of the 1957 Act provides that a banker is to be considered the holder of a cheque payable to order for which he has given value, or on which he has a lien, although the previous holder delivers it to him for collection without indorsing it.

If the cheque had been an order cheque, answer **c** would have been correct because a forged signature is totally inoperative and would therefore prevent the bank becoming the holder (true owner) of the cheque. However, the cheque could be a bearer cheque, in which case an indorsement, forged or otherwise, can be ignored, bearer cheques being negotiated by delivery alone.

So to the correct answer: to be the holder in due course of a cheque, the collecting bank must itself give value for it. Paying a cheque into an overdrawn account in the ordinary course of business does not constitute giving value — to do so it must be paid in specifically to reduce an existing overdraft.

Score 2 marks for each correct answer. What was your score for this topic? Fill it in on the score grid.

If you scored 12 or less and are still a bit shaky on some points go back and look at the study guide again, before proceeding any further.

If you are sure you really understand and are familiar with the topic now, try the 10 further questions which are on pages 193-195.

Alternatively you can go on to the next topic and do all the post-tests together at the end.

Post-tests

Pages 170-195 contain 10 further multiple choice questions for each topic.

Questions

Topic 1   Financial statements

1 Which of the following cases established the functional definition of banker:

  a *United Dominions Trust Ltd v. Kirkwood* (1966)?
  b *Ladbroke v. Todd*(1914)?
  c *Joachimson v. Swiss Banking Corporation* (1921)?
  d *Wood v. Martins Bank* (1951)?

2 In relation to the definition of a customer, *Ladbroke v. Todd* (1914) established that:

  a a course of dealings is necessary before a person becomes a customer of a bank.
  b a course of dealings is not necessary for a person to become a customer of bank.
  c a banker may owe legal duties to a person even though no account exists.
  d a banker owes a duty of secrecy to his customer about his affairs.

3 Which of the following cases established that a banker can owe a duty of good faith to his customer similar to that owed under a fiduciary relationship:

  a *Burnett v. Westminster Bank* (1966)?
  b *Tournier v. National Provincial and Union Bank of England* (1924)?
  c *Lloyds Bank v. Bundy* (1975)?
  d *Joachimson v. Swiss Banking Corporation* (1921)?

4 In relation to the repayment of an overdraft, *Williams & Glyn's Bank v. Barnes* (1980) established:

a the overdaft is always repayable on demand.
b the customer is always entitled to one month's notice before repayment can be demanded.
c the customer is always entitled to reasonable notice before repayment can be demanded.
d the customer may be entitled to reasonable notice before repayment can be demanded.

5 The rule in *London Joint Stock Bank v. Macmillan & Arthur* (1918) applies to:

a all types of negotiable instruments.
b all types of negotiable instruments that can be crossed.
c crossed cheques only.
d cheques only.

6 In which of the following situations can a banker still safely pay his customer's cheques:

a notice of a receiving order against a customer?
b the making of a winding up order against a customer?
c the issuing of a garnishee order nisi against the bank?
d notice of an act of bankruptcy by the customer?

7 A countermand of a cheque is effective:

a when the customer telephones his bank with an instruction not to pay the cheque.
b when a letter of countermand is posted.
c when a letter of countermand is received.
d when a letter of countermand comes to the banker's attention.

8 A banker's lien:

    a transfers ownership of the documents or goods over which it is exercised to the bank.

    b transfers possession of the documents or goods over which it is exercised to the bank.

    c only covers documents deposited for security purposes.

    d always gives the banker a right of sale.

9 The case which established the general exceptions to a banker's duty of secrecy to his customer was:

    a *Woods v. Martins Bank* (1959).

    b *Tournier v. National Provincial Bank of England* (1924).

    c *United Overseas Bank v. Jiwani* (1976).

    d *Baines v. National Provincial Bank Ltd.* (1927).

10 The principal of liability established in *Hedley Byrne & Co v. Heller Partners Ltd* (1963) is:

    a contractual.

    b based on the tort of negligence.

    c based on the tort of deceit.

    d for breach of a fiduciary duty.

Topic 2 The law of agency

1 When an agent makes a contract without disclosing his agency:

    a the principal is not bound by the transaction.

    b the principal can ratify the contract.

    c the other contracting party can sue the agent.

    d the principal is never liable on the contract.

2 In *Ashbury Railway Carriage Co v. Riche* (1875) it was held that:

    a a company cannot ratify a contract if it is in undisclosed principal.

    b a company cannot ratify an *ultra vires* contract.

    c a company cannot ratify a pre-incorporation contract.

    d a company cannot ratify a contract voidable for fraud.

 answer

3 *Greenwood v. Martins Bank Ltd* (1933) is an example of agency being created by:

    a an express contract.

    b implication.

    c operation of law.

    d estoppel.

 answer

4 *Boardman v. Phipps* (1967) is an example of an agent:

    a being able to delegate his task.

    b acting negligently.

    c allowing his own interests to conflict with those of his principal.

    d disobeying his principal's instructions.

 answer

5 An agent's right to be indemnified by his principal means that:

    a he can deduct his commission from any monies he owes to his principal.

    b his principal must compensate him for any losses incurred while performing his duties.

    c he has a lien on his principal's goods in his possession for commission owed to him.

    d his principal must not prevent him from earning his commission.

 answer

6 An agent is personally liable on a bill of exchange unless he clearly indicates that he acts on behalf of his principal by virtue of the Bills of Exchange Act 1882:

   a s.3.
   b s.24.
   c s.26.
   d s.29.

7 The principle of breach of warranty of authority was established in:

   a *Said v. Butt* (1920).
   b *Collen v. Wright* (1856).
   d *Kelner v. Baxter* (1866).
   d *Keighley Maxstead v. Durant & Co* (1901).

8 Which of the following ways of terminating agency could give rise to an action for breach of contract:

   a revocation by the principal?
   b mutual agreement?
   c frustration of the contract?
   d the death of the principal?

9 An agent with authority to draw cheques also has authority to:

   a draw other forms of bills of exchange.
   b indorse cheques.
   c charge his principal's property as security.
   d negotiate a new overdraft facility.

10 If a banker collects cheques for an agent drawn by that agent on his principal's account, he risks losing the protection of:

   a the Bills of Exchange Act 1882, s.60.
   b the Bills of Exchange Act 1882, s.80.

c the Cheques Act 1957, s.2.
d the Cheques Act 1957, s.4.

_answer_

Topic 3   Partnership

1 The Partnership Act became law in:

a 1882.
b 1890.
c 1893.
d 1898.

_answer_

2 The normal maximum number of members in a firm is:

a 10.
b 15.
c 20.
d there is no normal maximum number.

_answer_

3 The implied authority of a partner in a trading partnership does not extend to:

a drawing cheques.
b creating an equitable mortgage.
c signing bills of exchange.
d executing deeds.

_answer_

4 A retiring partner can avoid liability to existing clients for future debts by:

a novation.
b giving them actual notice of his retirement.
c publishing notice of his retirement in the *London Gazette*.

    d ensuring the partnership's current account is broken by the
    bank.

5 The death of a partner:

    a automatically dissolves the firm by virtue of the 1890 Act.
    b automatically dissolves the firm by virtue of the 1890 Act unless
    the partners decide otherwise.
    c gives grounds to seek a court order for dissolution.
    d only dissolves the firm if the partners decide it should do so.

6 When a firm is dissolved, the three sources of funds available to
meet any losses are: **i** the partners' separate assets; **ii** the firm's
capital; **iii** undrawn profits. These are applied in the following
order:

    a i, ii, iii.
    b i, iii, ii.
    c iii, ii, i.
    d iii, i, ii.

7 In which of the following cases was it established that a partner has
no implied authority to open an account for the firm in his name
only:

    a *Alliance Bank v. Kearsely* (1871)?
    b *Devaynes v. Noble* (1816)?
    c *Smith and Baldwin v. Barclays Bank Ltd* (1944)?
    d *Kendall v. Hamilton* (1879)?

8 The Civil Liability (Contribution) Act became law in:

    a 1968.
    b 1982.

c 1978.
d 1975.

9 A firm's account is £10,000 overdrawn and a partner retires. The account is not ruled off immediately as it should be and payments in total £5,000 and payments out total £5,000 by the time this is done. The retiring partner remains liable for:

a nothing.
b £5,000.
c £10,000.
d £15,000.

10 A receiving order is made against the firm of ABC & Co. The assets are £25,000 and the liabilities are £50,000. A has separate assets of £30,000 and separate debts of £25,000, B has separate assets of £25,000 and separate debts of £15,000 and C has separate assets of £20,000 and separate debts of £20,000. The firm's creditors therefore receive a dividend of:

a 50p in the pound.
b 75p in the pound.
c 80p in the pound.
d 100p in the pound.

Topic 4 Companies

1 A private company:

a must have a minimum authorized and allotted share capital of £50,000.
b must have a minimum of two directors.
c can have no share capital.
d must have a 'business certificate' before it can commence business.

2   A company's legal capacity to enter into a contract is determined by:

   a   the registrar's certificate issued under the Companies Act 1985, s.117.

   b   the *ultra vires* rule.

   c   its object clause.

   d   its directors in a general meeting.

3   The decision in *Introductions Ltd v. National Provincial Bank Ltd* (1970) established that:

   a   a banker can rely on the Companies Act 1985, s.35 to recover an *ultra vires* loan from a company.

   b   a banker cannot rely on the Companies Act 1985, s.35 to recover an *ultra vires* loan from a company.

   c   the power to raise finance is independent of other objects stated in its memorandum of association.

   d   the power to raise finance is not independent of other objects stated in its memorandum of association.

4   A case which illustrates the importance of ensuring that a company decision in which a bank has an interest is taken by a quorum of independent directors is:

   a   *Victors v. Lingard* (1927).

   b   *Panorama Development (Guilford) Ltd v. Fidelis Furnishing Fabrics Ltd* (1971).

   c   *Phonogram Ltd v. Lane* (1981).

   d   *International Sales Agencies Ltd and Another v. Marcus and Another* (1982).

5   A fixed annual dividend is paid to:

   a   debenture holders.

   b   preference shareholders.

c   ordinary shareholders.
d   deferred shareholders.

6   Which of the following courses of action/legal principles will not aid a banker who lends money to a company for an *ultra vires* purpose:

a   subrogation.
b   a tracing order.
c   a retrospective alteration of the objects clause.
d   enforcement of any third party charge.

7   The Rule in *Turquand's Case* (1856) states that:

a   a director of a company is personally liable on a contract he makes on behalf of the company which he knows to be *ultra vires*.
b   a person dealing with a company must ensure that the proposed transaction is consistent with its articles and memorandum but may assume that the transaction has been properly authorized.
c   provided it was sanctioned by its directors and entered into by the other party in good faith, an *ultra vires* contract can be enforced against a company.
d   in a company's unbroken current account, payments in will be appropriated in date order to payments out.

8   A puisne mortgage given as security by a company must be protected by registration under the Companies Act 1985, s.395 and:

a   a deposit of title deeds.
b   on the Register of Land Charges.
c   on the Land Register.
d   on the Local Land Charges Register.

9 Under the Insolvency Act 1985, s.104, a floating charge in favour of a person unconnected with the company will be invalidated if the company goes into liquidation within:

a   6 months of its creation.
b   9 months of its creation.
c   12 months of its creation.
d   18 months of its creation.

10 A company can wind up voluntarily if the company resolves to do so and:

a   three months' notice is given to the Registrar of Companies.
b   the resolution is filed with the Registrar of Companies within 14 days.
c   its directors can file a declaration of solvency.
d   there are no creditors secured by fixed charges.

Topic 5   Bankruptcy

1 How many acts of bankruptcy are there:

a   5?
b   8?
c   10?
d   12?

2 To present a bankruptcy petition, a creditor, or two or more creditors together, must be owed, after deducting any security held, at least:

a   £250
b   £500
c   £750
d   £1000.

3 A receiving order takes effect from the day:

   a of the act of bankruptcy on which it is based.
   b it is made.
   c it is advertised in the *London Gazette*.
   d it is registered at the Department of Trade.

 *answer*

4 Mr Y committed acts of bankruptcy on the following dates: (i) 10 January, (ii) 25 March, (iii) 1 April, (iv) 26 April, all in the same year. His account with Mantown Bank was overdrawn during this period and unsecured. Having been informed of the act of bankruptcy committed on 26 April, the bank presented a bankruptcy petition on 2 May. Assuming that he is adjudicated bankrupt, his trustee's title to his property would commence on:

   a i.
   b ii.
   c iii.
   d iv.

 *answer*

5 *Lloyds Bank v. Marcan* (1973) was an example of:

   a an assignment for the benefit of creditors under the Bankruptcy Act 1914, s.1.
   a a fraudulent preference under the Bankruptcy Act 1914, s.1.
   c a fraudulent preference under the Law of Property Act 1925, s.172.
   d a criminal bankruptcy order under the Criminal Justice Act 1972.

 *answer*

6 Between the presentation of a bankruptcy petition and the adjudication order, there are the following stages in the bankruptcy process:
     i meeting of creditors.
     ii public examination.
     iii receiving order.
     iv statement of affairs.
These take place in the order:

a   i, ii, iii, iv.
b   ii, iii, iv, i.
c   iii, iv, i, ii.
d   iv, i, ii, iii.

7   The protection of the Bankruptcy Act 1914, s.46 is lost when:

a   the debtor commits an act of bankruptcy.
b   the creditor knows that the debtor has committed an act of bankrtuptcy.
c   a bankruptcy petition is presented.
d   the creditor knows that a bankruptcy petition has been presented against the debtor.

8   Under the deeds of Arrangement Act 1914, an arrangement or composition embodied in a document: (i) must be registered with the Department of Trade within a specified period of its execution and (ii) the trustee must file a declaration within a specified time stating that a majority by value and number of creditors assent to it. These specified periods are:

a   i. 7 days, ii. 14 days.
b   i. 7 days, ii. 21 days.
c   i. 14 days, ii. 14 days.
d   i. 14 days, ii. 28 days.

9   *Re Dalton* (1962) is a decision on:

a   the Bankruptcy Act 1914, s.45.
b   the Bankruptcy Act 1914, s.46.
c   the Bankruptcy Act 1914, s.47.
d   the Bankruptcy (Amendment) Act 1926, s.4.

10   Restrictions on a debtor's account first become necessary when:

    a   the debtor commits an act of bankruptcy.
    b   the bank has notice of an act of bankruptcy.
    c   a bankruptcy petition is presented against the debtor.
    d   the bank has notice that a bankruptcy petition has been presented against the debtor.

Topic 6   Land and its use as security

1   The Law of Property Act became law in:

    a   1914.
    b   1925.
    c   1926.
    d   1952.

2   Which of the following can only be an equitable interest:

    a   restrictive covenant?
    b   grant of fishing rights for 20 years?
    c   lease?
    d   a charge creating a mortgage.

3   A puisne mortgage is a:

    a   legal mortgage of unregistered land protected by a deposit of title deeds.
    b   equitable mortgage of unregistered land protected by a deposit of title deeds.
    c   legal mortgage of unregistered land unprotected by a deposit of title deeds.
    d   equitable mortgage of unregistered land unprotected by a deposit of title deeds.

4 A puisne mortgage must be registered in the Land Charges Register as a:

   a class A charge.
   b class C charge.
   c class D charge.
   d class F charge.

5 Title to registered land is proved by:

   a an abstract of title.
   b a collection of title deeds.
   c the land certificate.
   d the Land Register.

6 A memorandum of deposit is taken by a bank when:

   a an equitable mortgage is executed.
   b a legal mortgage is executed.
   c a mortgage of registered land is executed.
   d a mortgage of unregistered land is executed.

7 Which of the following would you not expect to find in a bank mortgage form:

   a an all moneys clause?
   b a free will clause?
   c a continuing security clause?
   d a clause making the advance repayable on demand?

8 A mortgage of unregistered land accompanied by a deposit of title deeds:

   a cannot be registered at all.
   b can only be registered if it is equitable.

   c can only be registered if it is a second mortgage.

   d must be registered.

   *answer*

9 If notice of deposit of a land certificate is registered at the Land Registry. the Registrar must give the mortgagee a specified period of notice of any proposed dealings with the land. This period is:

   a 7 days.

   b 14 days.

   c 21 days.

   d 28 days.

   *answer*

10 Which of the following remedies is not a right *in rem*:

   a an action for the debt?

   b sale of the property?

   c appointment of a receiver?

   d foreclosure.

   *answer*

Topic 7 Life policies and stocks and shares

1 An insurable interest is most likely to be absent when a:

   a wife insures her husband.

   b father insures his daughter.

   c company insures it managing director.

   d guarantor insures the principal debtor.

   *answer*

2 The principle of *uberrima fides* applies to the:

   a proposer.

   b insurer.

c   proposer and the insurer.

d   proposer, insurer and any assignee.

3   If age is not 'admitted' in a life policy, this:

a   is a breach of the *uberrima fides* principles.

b   reduces the value of the policy.

c   entitles the company to withold payment until it is admitted.

d   entitles the company to withold payment altogether.

4   A banker will take an equitable mortgage of a life policy by:

a   a deposit of the policy.

b   a deposit of the policy supported by a memorandum of deposit.

c   an indorsement on the policy.

d   a separate deed of assignment.

5   A bank's legal mortgage of a life policy is discharged by:

a   a reassignment by deed.

b   an indorsement on the policy.

c   cancellation of the memorandum of deposit.

d   giving notice of the discharge to the issuing company.

6   Which of the following securities are not a National Savings Security:

a   National Savings Certificates?

b   Premium Savings Bonds?

c   gilts?

d   British Savings Bonds?

7   Title to bearer securities is transferred:

    a   by delivery.
    b   by delivery and indorsement of the securities.
    c   completion of a stock transfer form.
    d   taking a memorandum of deposit.

answer

8   A legal mortgage of registered stocks and shares is effected by:

    a   their deposit with the bank.
    b   their deposit with the bank supported by a memorandum of deposit.
    c   the mortgagee being registered as their holder.
    d   the mortgagee being registered as their holder supported by a memorandum of deposit.

answer

9   A mortgage of American and Canadian style certificates is effected by:

    a   transfer of the securities into the mortgagee's name.
    b   transfer of the securities into the mortgagee's name supported by a memorandum of deposit.
    c   pledge.
    d   pledge supported by a memorandum of deposit.

answer

10   Over which of the following securities can a legal mortgage be taken:

    a   Unit Trust Certificates?
    b   Building Society shares?
    c   National Savings Certificates?
    d   Premium Savings Bonds?

answer

Topic 8   Guarantees

1   The term surety is another term for the:

   a   guarantor
   b   creditor.
   c   debtor.
   d   indemnifier.

2   The Statute of Frauds became law in:

   a   1657.
   b   1667.
   c   1677.
   d   1687.

3   Which of the following would not be consideration for a guarantee:

   a   continuing an existing overdraft?
   b   extending the period of an existing overdraft?
   c   increasing the amount of an existing overdraft?
   d   withdrawing a demand for repayment of an existing overdraft.

4   Under a guarantee, a surety:

   a   incurs primary liability.
   b   incurs secondary liability.
   c   must have an interest in the contract between the debtor and
       creditor.
   d   cannot avoid liability on the grounds that the creditor accidently
       gave him wrong information about the nature of the debt he
       secured.

5   A bank guarantee given by two or more co-guarantors:

    a   imposes only joint liability on the co-guarantors.

    b   imposes only several liability on the co-guarantors.

    c   allows the bank to release one of the co-guarantors from his obligation without affecting its rights against the others.

    d   is still valid against those that sign if one of the co-guarantors dies before he is able to sign.

answer

6   A guarantor is:

    a   never entitled to know the exact amount of the overdraft secured.

    b   only entitled to know the exact amount of the overdraft secured if the guarantee is not being fully relied upon.

    c   only entitled to know the exact amount of the overdraft secured if the guarantee is being fully relied on.

    d   always entitled to know the exact amount of the overdraft secured.

answer

7   An attestation clause in a guarantee is associated with:

    a   an *ultra vires* clause.

    b   a guarantee given by two or more persons.

    c   a free will clause.

    d   a deposit of securities by the surety in support of the guarantee.

answer

8   Which of the following can never give a valid guarantee:

    a   a private company:

    b   a partnership?

    c   a married woman?

    d   a seventeen-year-old bank employee?

answer

9 The repayment of a guaranteed loan may occasionally constitute a fraudulent preference. To preserve its rights against the guarantor should this happen, the agreement will provide that the bank can hold the agreement uncancelled for a further period after repayment is made; this period is:

a three months.
b six months.
c nine months.
d twelve months.

answer

10 It is usual for a bank guarantee to require the surety to give a specified period of notice before determining the guarantee. This period is usually:

a one week.
b one month.
c three months.
d six months.

answer

Topic 9   Bills of exchange

1 Which of the following is not a bill of exchange:

a cheque?
b banknote?
c postal order?
d treasury bill?

answer

2 A bill of exchange is defined by the Bills of Exchange 1882:

a section 1.
b section 2.
c section 3.
d section 4.

answer

3   Which of the following would be invalid wording on a bill of exchange:

   a   pay A or B or order £5,000 on 30 June 1985?
   b   pay C or order £5,000 on 30 June 1986?
   c   pay D £5,000 in three equal instalments due 30 April 1986, 31 May 1986 and 30 June 1986 with interest at 10% per annum?
   d   pay E or order on the arrival of *SS Angelides* at Harwich?

 *answer*

4   An accommodation bill is one:

   a   to which there are only two parties.
   b   where the drawer is the payee.
   c   where no consideration is given for its acceptance.
   d   drawn by a parent company on one of its subsidiaries.

 *answer*

5   The definition of a holder in due course is found in the Bills of Exchange Act 1882:

   a   section 2.
   b   section 3.
   c   section 24.
   d   section 29.

 *answer*

6   Which of the following is not a party to a bill of exchange:

   a   the drawer?
   b   the acceptor?
   c   the payee?
   d   the indorser?

 *answer*

7   A draws a bill of exchange on B payable to C or order. The bill is stolen by D who forges C's indorsement and negotiates it to E who takes it as a holder in due course. E can enforce the bill against:

a   A, B, C and D.
b   B, C and D.
c   C and D.
d   D.

8   Which of the following statements is incorrect. An indorsement:

a   must be written on the back of the bill.
b   must be of the entire bill or of a specified part thereof.
c   if there are two or more payees, all must endorse, unless one is authorized to indorse for the others.
d   should correspond exactly with the drawing or previous indorsement.

9   Payment in due course discharges a bill of exchange. Such a payment can be:

a   before, at or after the bill's maturity.
b   before or after the bill's maturity.
c   before or at the bill's maturity.
d   at or after the bill's maturity.

10   Which of the following events discharges a bill of exchange:

a   payment to its holder three days before the due date for payment?
b   payment at the due date to a person in possession of a bearer bill?
c   the holder renouncing his rights against one or more parties to the bill?
d   when it is accidently torn up?

Topic 10   Cheques

1   A cheque is defined by the Bills of Exchange Act 1882:

   a   section 3.
   b   section 59.
   c   section 60.
   d   section 73.

 *answer*

2   A cheque is said to be 'stale' and a bank will usually not pay it when it has been in circulation for more than:

   a   3 months.
   b   6 months.
   c   9 months.
   d   12 months.

 *answer*

3   A crossing:

   a   is a material part of a cheque.
   b   is a direction to the collecting banker.
   c   is exclusive to cheques.
   d   cannot be altered.

 *answer*

4   An effective countermand of a cheque:

   a   can be made by telephone.
   b   must be made in writing.
   c   must be made in writing and must be received by the bank.
   d   must be made in writing and must come to the attention of the bank.

 *answer*

5   The protection afforded by the Rule in *London Joint Stock Bank v. Macmillan and Arthur* (1918) applies to:

   a   any bill of exchange.
   b   any cheque.

c   only crossed cheques.
d   any instrument that can be crossed.

6   Which of the following is not a requirement of payment in due
course of a cheque under the Bills of Exchange Act 1882, s.59; that
the payment must be:

a   to the holder?
b   according to the acceptance?
c   in good faith?
d   without notice of any defect in the holder's title?

7   Which of the following would prevent a banker relying on the Bills
of Exchange Act 1882, s.60:

a   payment of a cheque bearing a forged indorsement?
b   negligence?
c   payment of an open cheque over the counter?
d   payment of a crossed cheque over the counter?

8   Which of the following is the Cheques Act 1957, s.1 specifically
concerned with:

a   irregular indorsements?
b   forged indorsements?
c   unauthorized indorsements?
d   any indorsements?

9   To which of the following instruments does the Cheques Act 1957,
s.4 not apply:

a   bills of exchange other than cheques?
b   postal orders?

c dividend warrants?
d bankers' drafts.

10 *Midland Bank v. Reckitt* (1933) was an example of negligence in the collection of cheques by:

a failure to obtain the name of its customer's employer.
b crediting cheques payable to a company to the private account of an official of the company.
c crediting a private account of an agent or of an employee with cheques drawn by him on the account of his principal or employer.
d crediting an agent's private account with cheques expressly payable to him in his capacity as an agent.

Answers follow on pages 196-197. Score 2 marks for each correct answer.

Answers

Topic 1   Financial statements

1a	2b	3c	4d	5d
6d	7d	8c	9b	10b

Topic 2   The law of agency

1c	2b	3d	4c	5b
6c	7b	8a	9b	10d

Topic 3   Partnership

1b	2c	3d	4b	5b
6c	7a	8c	9b	10c

Topic 4   Companies

1c	2c	3d	4a	5b
6c	7b	8b	9c	10b

Topic 5   Bankruptcy

1c	2c	3b	4b	5c
6c	7d	8b	9b	10d

Topic 6   Land and its use as security

1b	2a	3c	4b	5d
6a	7b	8a	9b	10a

Topic 7   Life policies and stocks and shares

1b	2c	3c	4b	5a
6c	7a	8d	9b	10b

Topic 8   Guarantees

1a	2c	3a	4b	5c
6b	7c	8d	9b	10c

Topic 9   Bills of exchange

1c	2c	3d	4c	5d
6c	7d	8b	9d	10b

Topic 10   Cheques

1d	2b	3a	4d	5b
6b	7d	8a	9a	10c

Score Grid

Topic	Score ?/20	Revision campaign					
		Revision order 1–10	Study guide page no.	MCQs page no.	Score ?/20	Post test page no.	Score ?/20
1							
2							
3							
4							
5							
6							
7							
8							
9							
10							